# Loan Processing: Career Training

**A. Johnson – Johnson Publication**

2

# Loan Processing: Career Training
A. Johnson

---

**Johnson Publication**

This book is to provide easy career training for all those who are interested in becoming a mortgage loan processor. Our ultimate goal is to help the unemployed become employed- Our Easy Loan Processing: Career Training- can do just that!
ISBN 978-1-304-59841-7
PCN – Library of Congress Control number- 2013921377

# Easy Loan Processing: Career Training

ISBN 978-1-304-59841-7
PCN – Library of Congress Control number- 2013921377


Printed in the United State of America
© 2014 Johnson publications
Chicago, IL

Notification:

This Manual is intended for the sole purpose of Training/educating individuals or companies in the Mortgage field. This training manual focuses on the fundamental aspects of residential mortgage lending. The contents in this book are supposed current and accurate at the time of publishing. However, the information in this guide is subject to change without notice due to state law modifications. We take no responsibility for any due to any changes. Johnson Publications assumes no responsibility for any changes or inaccuracy that may occur within this industry. We strongly urge you to check periodically with Fannie Mae or Freddie Mac as well as other industries in this field for constant changes and updates. Each state and or individual company may have certain requirements not listed in this edition. We cannot be held liable for additional employment requirements by any company in any state due to changes in rules and laws. We strongly advise you to check with other mortgage companies within your own state.

Please note: within each lending institution, various laws and rules differ and change from time to time. This training guide cannot qualify you for any type of degree that may be required by your local state. Although there are currently no degree requirements for any loan processing position, this could at some point in time change?

Note: Some pages within this book have been intentionally left blank, blurred, changed or distorted to protect real information.

# Book Contents

**About this book**
The mortgage loan transaction trail
Section Terms

**Chapter One - Step One: The application**
What is a mortgage loan?
Pre-application

**Getting Started**
Witt the Loan Officer

**Chapter Two – Step Two: The Loan Officer and Loan Processor**
Receiving and reviewing loan application - 1003
The loan process

**Chapter Three- Step Three: After Pre-approval, then what?**
The Successful Processor
Simple analysis
Order the appraisal and title information

**Chapter Four- Step Four: Processing Underwriter's Package**
Stacking order
Underwriting - Checklist review
Submit

**Chapter Five- How to section**
Application breakdown- Step-by-step
How to get started DU- Desktop underwriting
Employment help

**Chapter Six**
Forms and Disclosures
Tips – Warnings

**Chapter Seven**
National Component Pre-test A-B-C
Glossary

# About this book:

Our easy career training is an instruction book covering above and beyond basic mortgage loan processing. Choosing our training guide is an excellent and inexpensive way to enter the mortgage profession. Loan Processors are in powerful demand these days, and can earn an exceptional income. Therefore, becoming a loan processor is a wise career choice. Your success will depend on your personal efforts and limitations, but your door of opportunity is knocking. We feel quite confident you will positively benefit from our easy step-by-step training guide. The ultimate goal for any instructor should be to move each processor forward easily and quickly. Our qualified instructors have specifically designed this training program to be short and uncomplicated as possible. This training guide will teach you beyond the basic in and outs of Loan Processing. This includes sample forms, glossary, mortgage terms and the National Component Prep Test, A and B. C. Soon, you will be well on your way to becoming a successful loan processor.

This book includes additional sections for employment interviewing, helpful tips and helpful tips and suggestions, warnings and an awesome glossary. At the risk of sounding presumptuous we are giving you one heck of a deal at this price. We have offered you all we can, now you have to take the first step, then keep walking! You can only grow from this point on. Please keep in mind, this is not a get-rich quick program; it's a career training. Every goal set for ones life can only be successfully achieved by applying dedication, training and hard work.

We have successfully condensed and simplified this manual down to seven basic steps for processing the mortgage loan, for your ease. After completing the first few sections of this manual, you should have a sufficient understanding of the mortgage loan process. Learning the language will help you intelligently communicate within the mortgage industry. Training any one individual to qualify for employment at all establishments in every state would be nearly impossible for any training guide. However, this book will definitely have you in the door of employment earning a nice income. Should you need or desire more help and research, you can download handbooks from numerous web sites on the Internet. Freddie Mac and Fannie Mae sites will help you in many areas in which you may need additional insight.

# Introduction

## So, you decided on a career as a Mortgage Loan Processor? Congratulations on your new career! You Can Do It!

The Loan processor plays a crucial role within the mortgage industry. The mortgage processor processes a borrower's loan application files. The processor does not find the actual loans or borrowers, nor do they approve them. They are the person who does the processing for the loan officer and the lender. Being a mortgage loan processor certainly is not an easy task. It can be quite challenging and a bit overwhelming when you don't fully understand the mortgage process. This is why we are making our book available to anyone who desires to be a loan processor. Successful loan processors are no different from you; they simply apply the principles and techniques taught here to develop their career. The best news, many of today's mortgage software programs make the task of loan processing easier than ever. You may later at some point decide to become a Loan Originator or possibly a Realtor, who knows? Getting your foot in the mortgage industry will open the door to a number of opportunities. While a college degree may not be mandatory to become a mortgage processor; the processors should have a sufficient knowledge about the industry.

Understanding the process and knowing the primary purpose of the loan will turn the overwhelming ordeal into ease in a short time. The first part of our guide explains the beginning steps to processing mortgage loans. This guide will help you through the opening loan process and will explain the people involved. It will help you with the forms you will be asked to compile. After you become familiar with the various documents required, the individuals involved, the terms and your specific duties of the mortgage process your task will seem much less intimidating. Therefore, after completing this section you should have a genuine understanding of the entire process and your personal duties. You then will be well on your journey toward your new career.

# The Mortgage Loan Transaction

## Mortgage Loan baseball

**We're going to demonstrate this like a game-.**
The following is not your training, but the mortgage loan file trail.

The ins and out – Mortgage Baseball

### 4   Key players in the next couple sections
Player 1 The Buyer/borrower - Player 2 - The Loan Officer
Player 3 –The Lender      Player 4 The Loan Processor

### Game rules – object of the game – Processing Mortgage Home Loans

Player 1, - The home buyer/borrowers to try to get financial help purchasing their newly found home, they would like to move to. The buyers cannot afford to pay cash for this home, so they will need to get a home loan (mortgage).

Step 1, Player 2 - They look for a dependable, trustworthy loan officer to help them obtain a mortgage. The loan officer gives them a loan application to complete. He or she will collect supporting documentation and runs a credit check on all borrowers to see whether they will qualify for financial help. The loan officer looks over the potential borrower's application; the credit report and other evidence then will make the determination if the borrowers qualify for a home loan mortgage?

Step 2,  If the loan officer should determine the potential borrowers pre-qualify for a mortgage loan, the loan office will give a pre-approval. The loan officer will then send the borrowers loan file with all the collected contents to the loan processor for further processing.

## SHOULD THE POTENTIAL BORROWERS NOT PRE-QUALIFY, GAME OVER.

Step 3, Player 4- The loan processor takes the file with the signed application, supporting documentation, verifications, title, appraisal and other required documents they have been requested to collect and enters it carefully into a company database. After all important require loan documents have been collected, and entered correctly into the company database, the loan processor submits the entire file contents to underwriting for final approval.

Step 4, Player 3 - Underwriting receives the potential borrowers loan file and makes a vital determination if they are responsible enough to qualify for a mortgage loan?

Step 5, Player 4- If and when the loan processor receives an approval for the borrowers from underwriting, the loan processor will then schedule a closing date. Note: Often times, underwriting will find the potential borrowers qualify, but require more supporting documentation or evidence. This is called underwriting conditions.

Step 6, Player 4– The loan processor will speedily collect the underwriters conditions. The loan processor will enter the information into the database and send to underwriting for final approval and closing date for the borrowers.

Step 7, The Closing - When underwriting has given loan approval to the borrowers, the loan processor will then schedule a closing date to close the file and fund the borrowers loan so the can take possession of their home.

There are other players involved in this game, but they will appear after the first home run. At this time, bases are loaded. ☺

Mortgage Loan baseball

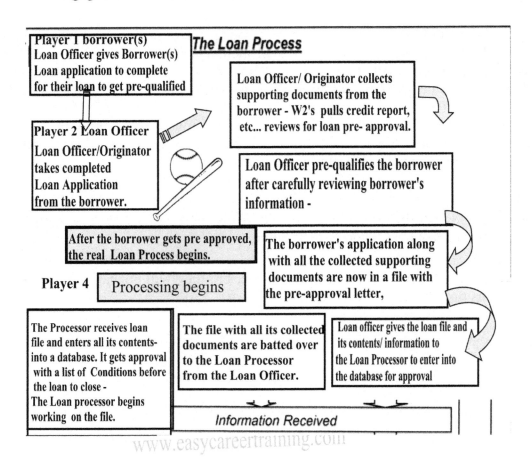

**The Loan Process**

Player 1 borrower(s)
Loan Officer gives Borrower(s)
Loan application to complete
for their loan to get pre-qualified

Loan Officer/ Originator collects
supporting documents from the
borrower - W2's pulls credit report,
etc... reviews for loan pre- approval.

Player 2 Loan Officer
Loan Officer/Originator
takes completed
Loan Application
from the borrower.

Loan Officer pre-qualifies the borrower
after carefully reviewing borrower's
information -

After the borrower gets pre approved,
the real Loan Process begins.

The borrower's application along
with all the collected supporting
documents are now in a file with
the pre-approval letter,

Player 4    Processing begins

The Processor receives loan
file and enters all its contents-
into a database. It gets approval
with a list of Conditions before
the loan to close -
The Loan processor begins
working on the file.

The file with all its collected
documents are batted over
to the Loan Processor
from the Loan Officer.

Loan officer gives the loan file and
its contents/ information to
the Loan Processor to enter into
the database for approval

*Information Received*

10

1, Buyer finds home through a realtor.
2, Buyer finds trustworthy Loan Officer to apply for Mortgae Loan.
3, Loan Officer collects personal and financial data from the borrower,
 reviews  loan application and pulls a credit report.
4, Loan Officer reviews buyer's application and pre qualifies the buyer.
5, Loan Officer seeks suitable lender to approve and agree to fund
the buyer's home loan.

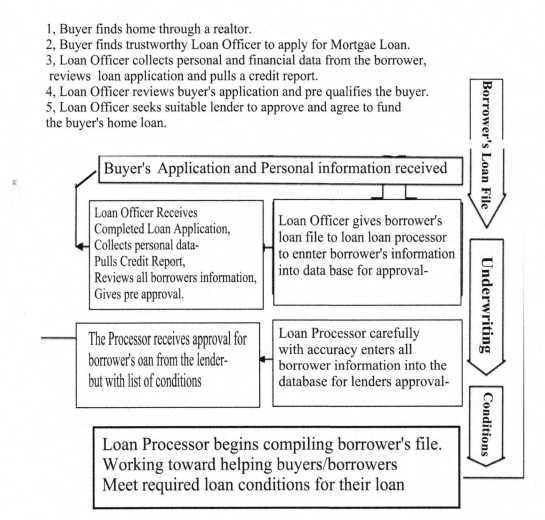

Players 1, 2, 3, 4   let's play ball!

**Ok, lets get started!**

# Section Terms

- **Buyer(s) or Borrower** - who are in the process of buying a home.
- **Co-Borrower** – any additional person that may be responsible for loan repayment and is listed on the title.
- **Application** - An initial statement of personal and financial information that is required to approve your loan.
- **Property** – Something owned - A piece of real estate.
- **Real Estate** - Land, including all the natural resources and permanent buildings on it.
- **Lender** – Someone who makes funds available to another with the expectation that the funds will be repaid, plus any interest and/or fees. A lender can be an individual, or a public or private group. Lenders may provide funds for a variety of reasons, such as a mortgage, automobile loan or small business loan.
- **Mortgage** – AKA Mortgage Note- mortgage note is legal evidence of your indebtedness and your formal promise to repay the debt. It sets out the amount and terms of the loan and also recites the penalties and steps the lender can take if you fail your payments on time.
- **Loan** - money borrowed that is usually repaid with interest.
- **File** - A collection of papers or published materials kept or arranged in convenient order.
- **Conditions** - Standard- when a loan is approved, it will be approved based on certain loan conditions or loan contingencies. Some loan conditions are standard for all loans, such as the condition that you buy hazard insurance in the amount of the mortgage loan and name the lender as an insured party on the policy. Other conditions may be specific to your loan.
- **Closing** - The end or conclusion - the final phase of a transaction, esp. the sale of real estate.
- **Underwriting** - the process of analyzing a loan application to determine the amount of risk involved in making the loan; it includes a review of the potential borrower's credit history and a judgment of the property value.
- **Loan Processor** –The person responsible for putting the borrower's file information into a systematic order, and submitting to underwriting.
- **Loan Officer** - a representative of a lending or mortgage company who is responsible for soliciting homebuyers, qualifying and processing of loans. They may also be called lender, loan representative and account executive or loan rep.

# Chapter One

## What is a mortgage loan?

**Mortgage Loan:**
A debt instrument, secured by the collateral of specified real estate property, that the borrower is obliged to pay back with a predetermined set of payments. Individuals, and businesses when making a large real estate purchase without paying the entire value of the purchase up front use mortgages. Over a period of many years, the borrower repays the loan, plus interest, until he/she eventually owns the property free and clear. Mortgages are also known as "liens against property" or "claims on property." If the borrower stops paying the mortgage, the bank can foreclose.

**Pre-Application - A Prospective borrower:**
**Financial help to purchase real estate-**
When a person or business decides to stop renting or moves to another state, they usually purchase a home or other piece of property. Buying a home or any investment property is probably one of the biggest decisions that people make daily. The average person cannot afford to pay cash for their home or business, so they need financial assistance. The first step an individual should make when not having the funds to purchase real estate, is contacting a lender to apply for a loan. The lender or loan officer and some cases with various companies, the loan processor can help them apply for financial assistance. They can apply for a Mortgage (loan) through a financial institution or filling out a loan application online. A number of individuals may also decide to refinance their existing property or purchase a second home for various reasons?

The process of applying for a mortgage loan can be a stressful process if not adequately researched by the borrowers. Often times the borrowers focus on moving into their home opposed to the process involved. The borrower should know what type of home is desired and what his or her budget will allow. This may determine the type of mortgage they should acquire. It is important for the borrower to acquire a copy of their credit report and check it for errors before beginning this process. If there are any inconsistencies, they can be disputed and possibly removed. This would save a lot of time and energy for everyone involved throughout the loan process, but many homebuyers focus mainly on their desired home.

**Step One – Application - Beginning Borrower's File -**
**When a borrower applies for a home loan: (Mortgage)**

It takes a team of loan specialist to assist a borrower in obtaining financial help, or a mortgage loan. Each specialist has an important task that must be performed correctly in order to carry out this process. It's likened unto that of an emergency room or operating room. The initial meeting with the loan officer and borrowers will consist of completing a loan application. The Loan Officer will give the potential borrower/buyer a loan application to try to get them pre-qualified. The loan application, also known as a 1003 contains all the borrower/ buyer's personal data and financial information. Just because a potential borrower completes a loan application does not necessary guarantee a mortgage loan. The loan applicant must meet all the guidelines before accepted and approved by a lender before the file closes, and the borrowers get the funds needed. Within some companies, the loan processor may have the opportunity or task of assisting the borrower with the application.

Along with the information on the application, the borrowers will need to supply a considerable amount of supporting documentation. The loan officer will ask for income verification and other asset documentation. The Loan officer or processor will request copies of driver's licenses on all borrowers. Original social security cards with the social security numbers (not a copy) so the borrower's credit record can be accessed. The loan officer will request the borrower's credit report so their FICO scores and credit history can be analyzed. Without the proper information and documentation, the lender will not and cannot approve the borrowers for a loan. The borrowers must cooperate by completing the loan application and providing the requested documents in a well-timed manner. After completing the buyer's application and collecting supporting documents such as w2s, credit report and other financial information the loan officer will make a predetermined judgment about the borrowers' pre-qualification and amount of loan the borrowers qualify for. The loan officer and lender will work with the borrowers to find the best loan options to suit their personal needs. In some companies, the loan processor will also be involved in this process.

When the borrowers have completed their application, and various supporting documents have been collected, the loan officer or lender will determine the borrower's risk factor and may give them a pre-qualification status or pre-approval letter. The borrower's loan application can move forward when the    lending guidelines have been met. The borrower must have an acceptable FICO credit score and prove they have sufficient means for repaying the loan.

If any issues arise from this review, such as bankruptcies or late payments, the loan officer, lender or processor works with the client to get additional explanations for the issue and submit them with the file.    The loan officer or lender will forward the borrower's pre-qualified file to the loan processor, who will continue processing the loan file.

**Important note:** The Loan Officer and the Lender are not the same.

There are many borrowers who begin their loan application process online. The online applications usually go to the lender and then forward to in-house loan officer or processor.

**Important note:** Just because the loan officer pre-qualifies the borrowers does not mean they are **approved**, they're only **pre-qualified**. The loan officer does not have the authority or responsibility of approving loans. They are only able to give a predetermined judgment. Only can the financial institution lender can give final loan approval.

| | |
|---|---|
|  | General list of documents needed to begin the borrower's loan process. These documents are collected into a file for the borrower's loan.<br><br>• Loan Application- 1003<br>• Copy borrower's drivers licenses<br>• Bank information - With borrowers names, address, account numbers, and three months of statements.<br>• W-2s - two years<br>• Proof of employment and worth of income.<br>• Employment Pay stubs – Sixty days<br>• Child Support - if applicable<br>• Any other income that would be used to pay back loan<br>• Three months of investment statements.<br>• Tax returns and balance sheets for the self-employed.<br>• Debt currently owed, including amounts due and account numbers.<br><br>Divorce papers if applicable? |

# Chapter Two

## Loan Officer and Loan Processor

**Step Two –**
**The Loan Officer-**
Once lending guidelines have been satisfied, the Lender or the Loan Officer will use the borrower's completed signed application, their verifications and disclosures to create a chosen stacking order. This file goes to the loan processor to finish the compiling for underwriting.

### The Loan Processing
The Loan processor plays a crucial role within the mortgage industry. The mortgage processor begins processing a borrower's loan application files after the loan officer or the lender has given a pre-approval or pre-qualification. The processor does not actually recruit the borrower's loans, nor do they approve them. They are the individual who does the processing for the loan officer and the lender.

### The Loan Processor
As the processor, you will have a great deal of interactions between the <u>borrowers, the Loan Officer and the lender</u>. You will also mediate between the <u>borrower and underwriting</u>. Although you may never meet with the underwriting team, you will have a lot of interactions with them. There are other individuals you will interact with as well during this loan process. At this point, in the book, let's focus on the processing software and initial step for entering borrower's application and documentation.

### The loan processors function within the industry.

The primary function of the Loan Processor is to ensure the timely and accurate packaging of all borrowers' loans originated by the loan officer, or lender. Once the processor receives the borrower's file, he or she will thoroughly review it for complete and accurate information and documentation. The processor will continue to compile the file and prepare it for underwriting submittal. An important function of the loan processor is the responsibility for requesting, and coordinating numerous additional supporting documents. The main focal point of the processor is to gather each file's information, taking them from pre-approval to closing. The documentation in the borrower's file has significant importance that's entrusted to the loan specialist, especially the processor. The processor is to ensure they are completed, accurate, and verified, and they comply with company policy. All borrowers' loan documents, including income validation, credit report, appraisal and title insurance must be collected, verified and packaged in a precise stacking order before a lender receives them. The processor must make sure all the documents required for the loan file are present and signed, while meeting crucial deadlines.

They also perform any additional duties/activities assigned by management.

The term Loan processor will take on different tasks or purposes depending on the institution you work for, and its size. The typical scenario is, the larger the company, the more specialized the job becomes. You will learn what the term Loan processor can represent, and the duties required within that company. The loan processor is often the main point of contact for borrowers after the loan officer. The overall job of a loan processor, in a nutshell, is to assist the loan officers in getting the borrower's mortgage loan compiled into a packaged stacking order, approved, submitted to underwriting and closed. Again, to get the borrower's loan approved and closed in a timely manner is of the essence. The loan processor ensures all the borrower's file contents are collected, verified and accurately entered into the database. Any missing documentation or inaccurate information will cause a delay, even worse, a loan denial. Many times, the workload will consume a good part of the day, with few breaks. There are certain traits expected of a person to be an outstanding loan processor. A good loan processor meets all deadlines for the borrower lone file to close.

**Certain qualities a must-**
To be successful as a loan processor, the person must be diligent at their work and have an eye for detail. They are expected to analyze the documents and carry out the calculations with a lot of care. The loan processor is required to have outstanding communication and organizational skills. They should display a pleasing personality when dealing with other individuals involved. They should be, or must become computer literate.
**Success is not only learned, but also earned.**

One very important quality any individual should possess in this Industry or any other trade is confidence. If you lack confidence within yourself, you certainly will not be capable of successfully convincing an employer to entrust his or her business in your hand. You must believe in yourself in order to succeed in anything in life. Confidence is most important for a loan processor; this person is often responsible for how fast the entire process goes.
**DO NOT let all this deter you!** Like all new things, it may seem like a lot at first, but then it's just another everyday thing.

**The automated software database:**
When processing mortgage loans, it is mandatory to learn the company's mortgage processing software. This will be, or should be already installed on company computer

for you. Your company should give set up a login for you and get you started. Most mortgage companies use Calyx Point, DU, LOS or Loan Ace. These software programs differ, but all serve the same function and offer the identical forms. Here's some good news for you; you can learn the software online at your own leisure before applying for any position. Loan Ace offers free mortgage processing software training on its company website as well as tons of resources on the others. Fannie Mae and Freddie Mac web sites have more information than you will ever need for any job to do with mortgages. They also offer every form needed to view or train. Please see the books resource section in chapter six.

I have yet more encouraging news for you. The software most companies use these days will help make your processing task so much easier. Several years' back, processors processed the borrower's loans manually, but now it's mainly automated. It's a matter of learning the software and going through the pages entering the information.

**Tip:** You will do yourself a lot of good by researching and learning the various software for loan underwriting and processing.

You can go to this website and check out some training.
Calyx Training Center- Training and resources offered-
**ORIGINATING & PROCESSING:**

Topics Covered -http://www.calyxsoftware.com/
Pre-qualifying your prospect
Converting the file from Prospect to Borrower
Overview of the Loan Application (including GFE & TIL)
Saving time with Cardex
Submitting to Fannie Mae & Freddie Mac
Printing & Emailing
Using Task Manager to keep track of "to-do's"

**Processing and Verification continuation:**
The processor has already been processing the borrowers application files and verifying the all the information provided. Let's talk about the borrower's credit report that should be in your file. If the report is not in your file, please ask the loan officer if they have it for you? This report is extremely important for the borrower's file and underwriting to approve this loan. When and if you have the borrower's credit report, it must be verified for signature(s) and should include a borrower's credit report authorization and release form.

Next, let's talk about the importance of checking the borrower's application information. The information on the borrower's application is maybe one of the most important pieces of documentations in this file.

**Understanding the loan application – Form 1003 – See how to section.**
The borrower's loan application has ten vital sections to it; each is equally important. The first part of the uniform residential loan application, also known as from 1003 contains the information about the type of loan program and it's terms. The next section of the application contains the information about the property and purpose for the loan. The next section is vital personal information concerning the borrower or borrowers and co-borrowers if any. The next section concerns the financial information for all the borrowers involved in the loan. The fourth section of the loan application contains important employment data on all the borrowers. The fifth section is about the borrower's monthly income and combined housing expenses. The sixth section contains all the borrower's assets and liabilities. Section seven contains the details of transaction, and section eight contains declarations. The section nine is acknowledgement and agreements of the loan, and section ten is all about the government information and signatures and dates of the borrowers and interviewer (Loan officer or lender).

Every bit and piece of the borrower's application information is vital to the loan process. Without proper signatures, addresses, phone numbers and other loan approval factors, there would be no loan closing for this borrower.

# Chapter Three

## After pre-approval, then what?

### Step Three –The Successful loan processor

Numerous supporting documents are collected on all the borrower(s) at the initial meeting, but the loan process requires many more. These documents are to help convince the lender; the borrowers are responsible individuals and not a bad financial risk. Your role as a Loan Processor is a very important during the entire loan process.

### Receiving and reviewing file

Upon receiving the borrower's loan file from the Loan Officer or Originator, the loan processor will begin compiling the loan documents creating a particular stacking order. See sample below - In your file, you should have been given the following documents. In general, the mortgage processor checks and verifies the entire package as given by the lender or loan officer.

### Simple Analysis

**A simple analysis on each file will save you and everyone else a lot of time.** When a lender or loan officer pre-qualifies the borrowers for the loan, they will forward the loan application file to the loan processor. The loan processor then becomes the borrower's mediator in the loan process. It is to everyone's advantage to get the borrower's loan closed. The loan officer assembles the documents in borrower's file, and reviews the file with two things in mind: Does the borrower indeed qualify for the type of loan they want, and will it pass smoothly through the underwriting process? Essentially, the loan officer must "pre-underwrite" the loan to make sure it will be closed for the borrowers. Although, everything may look like a smooth ride at this point, many borrowers experience some difficulty during the loan process. The processor will often contact the borrower requesting additional documentation needed to complete the loan file to submit to the underwriter. Underwriting is careful not to let anything in question get pass them. The best remedy for this backlash is to keep on top of all documentation, signatures and verifications.

### Checking the beginning file contents – File Compiling
1. Borrower's completed -Signed Mortgage Loan Application 1003-
2. Written Pre-approval letter for the loan-
3. The credit report - indicating borrower's FICO score-
4. W2 or W2 s for all borrowers
5. Borrower (s) Pay Stubs
6. Gift Letter  (if borrower is receiving a financial gift)
7. 2 most recent bank statements

8. Other Various Disclosures

**First and very important, carefully check the borrower's application** and enter the information into the company's loan-processing database. Include copies of the original application, two-year tax returns, two months pay stubs and two months bank statements for each loan.

It's good practice to check the file right away, making notes of any missing forms or information, advising the loan officer and borrowers immediately.

Step-by-Step breakdown of the loan application – 1003
see how to section of the book- You can download a free form from the HUD or Freddie Mac web site - Search hud clips

## Uniform Residential Loan Application

This application is designed to be completed by the applicant(s) with the Lender's assistance. Applicants should complete this form as "Borrower" or "Co-Borrower," as applicable. Co-Borrower information must also be provided (and the appropriate box checked) when [ ] the income or assets of a person other than the Borrower (including the Borrower's spouse) will be used as a basis for loan qualification or [ ] the income or assets of the Borrower's spouse or other person who has community property rights pursuant to state law will not be used as a basis for loan qualification, but his or her liabilities must be considered because the spouse or other person has community property rights pursuant to applicable law and Borrower resides in a community property state, the security property is located in a community property state, or the Borrower is relying on other property located in a community property state as a basis for repayment of the loan.

If this is an application for joint credit, Borrower and Co-Borrower each agree that we intend to apply for joint credit (sign below):

Borrower          Co-Borrower

### I. TYPE OF MORTGAGE AND TERMS OF LOAN

| Mortgage Applied for: | ☐ VA  ☒ Conventional  ☐ Other (explain): | ☐ FHA  ☐ USDA/Rural Housing Service | Check one | Agency Case Number 000012111 ? | Lender Case Number 000012111 ? |
|---|---|---|---|---|---|
| Amount $ 199,999 ? | Interest Rate 4 ? % | No. of Months 360 ? | Amortization Type: ☒ Fixed Rate  ☐ GPM  ☐ Other (explain):  ☐ ARM (type): | Check one | |

### II. PROPERTY INFORMATION AND PURPOSE OF LOAN

| Subject Property Address (street, city, state & ZIP) | | No. of Units |
|---|---|---|
| Legal Description of Subject Property (attach description if necessary) | | Year Built |

| Purpose of Loan ☒ Purchase  ☐ Construction  ☐ Other (explain): Check one  ☐ Refinance  ☐ Construction-Permanent | Property will be Check one ☒ Primary Residence  ☐ Secondary Residence  ☐ Investment |
|---|---|

Complete this line if construction or construction-permanent loan.

| Year Lot Acquired | Original Cost | Amount Existing Liens | (a) Present Value of Lot | (b) Cost of Improvements | Total (a + b) |
|---|---|---|---|---|---|
| | $ | Complete this section if applicable to borrower | | $ | $ 0.00 |

Complete this line if this is a refinance loan.

| Year Acquired | Original Cost | Amount Existing Liens | Purpose of Refinance | Describe Improvements ☐ made  ☐ to be made | |
|---|---|---|---|---|---|
| | $ | $ | Complete this section if applicable to borrower | Cost: $ | |

| Title will be held in what Name(s) Complete Full names all borrowers | Manner in which Title will be held Individual - Jointly | Estate will be held in: ☐ Fee Simple ☐ Leasehold (show expiration date) |
|---|---|---|
| Source of Down Payment, Settlement Charges, and/or Subordinate Financing (explain) Complete this section | | |

**Tip:** If you have purchased a home and have your documents, use your personal file for hands-on training or familiarizing yourself with the various documents and forms.

The loan processor reviews the borrower's credit report, verifying their credit history in terms of debts and payments. The lender can tell much about the borrower responsibility by their credit and payment history. In case the processor discovers a bruised credit history such as late payments, bankruptcy, etc. he or she contacts the borrower and requests a written letter of explanation. Sometimes this can help the borrowers, and sometimes it will not. It depends on the type of bruise and the lender. If it's a delinquent payment, many times the applicant can settle the issue, and the receipt will be sufficient.

**Tip:** It's good practice to keep notes on the borrowers for underwriting of credit report findings rather they are excellent or poor. It's also good practice to note the three different credit scores.

Example: Trans union 725   Equifax 715   Experian 740

**Entering and Ordering supporting documentations**
Setting up and Using DU – Desktop Underwriting
You may also hear D.O.  Desktop originator

The loan processor will carefully analyze the borrower's loan information and documentation entering it into the company's database using a software known as DU or DO.  The name of the software may vary, but they serve the same purpose and have the identical results. The mortgage software is a type of Dashboard system. It's functions serve the same purpose as any program's dashboard.  If you have an eBay account, paypal, craigslists or any other account, you're e already using some type of dashboard and are a head of the game. When checking a car's dashboard, you can view many of the car's functions as well and the cars malfunctions. The mortgage dashboard system is not much different. It only has different categories, functions and information.  The dashboard tells you when you need to fill up and alerts you to any malfunctions. You will find the mortgage loan software can help you in the same ways.

**See the how to section for basic training help for the DU –**
If you would like to learn the software used by the processor, loan officer and underwriting, it's known as DU (desk-top top underwriting). Please check this out; it would be a tremendous help clarifying the process.

We have also included a list of related functions that you can get help and train to increase your mortgage knowledge.  You can learn these related functions on youtube.com qualifying you basically for any job dealing with mortgage loans. Learning these areas will open the door wide to a number of opportunities. Our only limit is within ourselves.

Note: The following steps were taken partly from the training help section on the Fannie Mae website – If you would like to learn more, we suggest you check out their learning and training section.
https://www.fanniemae.com/singlefamily/originating-underwriting-learning-center  You can learn everything you every wanted to know.

**Documents you will need to order/request**
The mortgage processor also orders or requests the <u>appraisal</u> and <u>title</u> and checks for property issues requiring further justifications.
Note: Again, keep in mind each office may require different responsibility from the processor-

**Ordering or requesting-**
**The Appraisal - Title information - Other documents.**

A title search must be completed on the borrower's property prior to the mortgage loan closing. Therefore the loan processor is required to order/request the title. The properties title will identify any liens that have been recorded against the property, search the records at the courthouse to make sure the seller of the property has sole ownership and the legal right to sell the property, and verify that all title and deed conveyances are in order. Once these items are cleared and verified, title insurance may be issued on the property that insures the owner and mortgage company against any claims on the property.  The lender or loan processor will also order or request the appraisal for the borrower's property.  When the loan processor or other loan specialist receives the appraisal of the property and this appraisal determines the market value of the home, which is used for collateral in the loan. **Note:** The borrower is charged a fee for the appraisal service and is usually included in the closing costs.

Mortgage lending companies and financial institutions usually already have a preferred company they use for requesting the title and appraisal for all their loans. This is not something the processor will need to decide. You only have to order or request it from them. This is also done on the automated mortgage software database.  Please be sure to check out the websites mentioned above for information and basic training.
**Collect and package all signed verifications and disclosures-**
**Order or request any missing documentation from the list (if applicable).**

1.  Title  (order quickly so you get it first) • Title Policy (this request goes out to the Title Company) – Turn around times may vary depending on the Title Company and the subject property. Normally 2-5 days
2.  Appraisal  (order quickly so you get it first) Usually a market analysis on an appraisal to see if the value is there before it became a loan. The Appraisal

(ordered through an affiliated ordering team) – turn around time is usually 1-2 weeks. Two reports are required for loan amounts over 1 million– completed by the appraiser and turned in with the appraisal report.

3.  VOE   verification of employment - this request goes out to you employer to complete – Turn around time depends on your Employer.
4.  VOD   verification of deposit  - this request goes out to your Bank to complete – Turn around time depends on your Bank
5.  VOM   Verification of Mortgage
6.  VOR   verification of rent (if borrower was a renter)  Rent schedule (Investment properties only)
7.  Home Owners Insurance
8.  Pay off if it's a refinance
9.  If Purchase  *Sales Contract:  Required prior to processing the loan
10.  Flood Certification (this is order through a computer system) – Turn around time is instantly
11.  Insurance Policy (this request goes out to your Insurance Agent) Turn around times may very depending on your Insurance Agent. Normally 2-3 days
12.  Condo Approval if applicable (Condo units only, this request goes out to the Condo Association to complete) – There are usually cost involved with this request that are responsibility of the borrower. Turn around time depends on the Condo Association. Normally 3-5 days.

**Additional verifications:**
• Social Security verification (this request is sent out to the Social Security Administration)  - Turn around time is 1-2 days
• 4506t Form (this request goes out to the IRS) Used to verify income. Turn around time is 2-3 days
• Fraud Guard (this is order through a computer system) – Turn around time is instantly
• Credit Report (this is requested through a computer system, normally at the begging of the process) – Turn around time is instantly
• Credit Supplements (this is requested through the credit agencies) – Used to bring any credit account up-to-date – Turn around time is 2-4 days

**Please refer to the forms and verifications section for sample forms**
**Also see the How to section for help.**

**Note:** A Sales Contract or Copy of it should be a part of the file given to you by the LO, if not, you must obtain the Signed Sales contract through the Realtor, Borrower or you can get the Borrower's Attorney's phone number and ask him or her for a copy of the signed document After receiving the sales contract, you will then need to check for the following *MUST BE SIGNED BY ALL PARTIES *

---

**Processing Tools Basic tools to begin work:**

☐ Computer
☐ Computer software
☐ Internet connection
☐ Laser printer/scanner
☐ Fax machine
☐ E-mail address
☐ Web page
☐ Copy machine
☐ Telephone
☐ Calculator
☐ Dictionary & thesaurus
☐ Desk calendar
☐ Self-stick and removable note pads
☐ Contact database
☐ Highlighter pens
☐ Pens, pencils, staple remover, tape, scissors, glue stick, stapler, etc.

---

## Section Terms

### 1003- Uniform residental loan application

**Underwriting:** The process of evaluating a loan application to determine the risk involved for the lender. Underwriting involves an analysis of the borrower's creditworthiness and the quality of the property itself.

**Underwriter package:** a complete package containing important documentation on or about a borrower before obtaining a loan.

**DU- Desktop Underwriting -** A particular computerized system for doing automated underwriting.

**Stacking Order:** requiring electronic loan delivery in specific **stacking orders**, electronic-document management is rapidly becoming a must-have for lenders,

**Appraisal:** A written analysis or opinion of the estimated value of a property prepared by a qualified appraiser. Contrast with home inspection.

**Title:** A legal document evidencing a person's right to or ownership of a property.

**Title Company:** A company that specializes in examining and insuring titles to real estate.

**Title insurance:** Insurance that protects the lender (lender's policy) or the buyer (owner's policy) against loss arising from disputes over ownership of a property.

**Title Search:** A check of the title records to ensure that the seller is the legal owner of the property and that there are no liens or other claims outstanding.

**Note:** A legal document that obligates a borrower to repay a mortgage loan at a stated interest rate during a specified period of time.
**Assets:** Anything of monetary value that is owned by a person. Assets include real property, personal property, and enforceable claims against others (including bank accounts, stocks, mutual funds, and so on).

**Underwriting Conditions:** Once borrower's home loan is approved, the underwriter will inform you that the loan is approved, however, based on a few conditions.

**Good Faith Esitmate (GFE):** The form that lists the settlement charges the borrower must pay at closing, which the lender is obliged to provide the borrower within three business days of receiving the loan application.

**TIL:** Truth-in-Lending disclosure - a government-required summary of the main terms and features of the mortgage loan the borrowers are obtaining.
http://www.mortgageknowledgebase.com/glossary - term423

**LTV:** Loan-to-value- is the ratio of how much you borrow compared to the value of the home you're borrowing against. It is calculated as the home value divided by the amount borrowed.

**COE:** Certificate of Eligibility

**VOD:** Verification of Deposit- A Verification of Deposit (VOD) is a document signed by the borrower's bank or other financial institution verifying the account balance and history. Usually required by lenders to verify borrower has the amount of money he/she claims on the 1003.
**VOE:** Verification of Employment- A Verification of Employment (VOE) is a document signed by the borrower's employer verifying his/her starting date, job title, salary, probability of continued employment and probability of future overtime.
**VOR:** Verification of Rent, which is completed by your landlord to verify that all of the rent is paid and that there haven't been any late payments (usually for 12 months)
**VOM:** Verification of Mortgage- is form used to verify the existing balance and monthly payments, and to check for any late payments on the account.

**Type of loans-**
**VA loan:** (also known as a Veterans Affairs Loan) is a mortgage loan guaranteed by the U.S. Department of Veterans Affairs.

**Conventional loan:** A home mortgage that is neither FHA-insured nor VA-guaranteed.

# Chapter Four-
## Processing Underwriter's Package

**Step four – The Underwriter package**

Underwriting is the department in lending that evaluates the loan documentation and determines whether or not the loan is within the guidelines, and the borrowers qualify for funding. It is the underwriter's responsibility to assess the risk of the loan and decide to approve or decline the loan. The processor is the one who completes and submits the borroer's loan documents to the underwriter. Underwriters take at least 48 hours to underwrite the loan after the processor sends them the borrower signed application with the packaged file. The normal turnaround for the processor to compile and package the file contents is between 10-15 days. The entire process from application to close can take from 5-35 days to process the loan.

There have been loans that close in as little as 15 days if the borrower wants an early close, and everything is good to go.

**Underwriters love a Cover Letter.**

If you want your underwriter to adore you and your loan files, I highly recommend you get in the habit of composing and submitting a cover letter with your file. It would be a really good practice to jot down many notes on your loans overviews on a consistent basis. Providing the underwriter with a quick overview of the file might take a few extra minutes of your time, but doing so will render you worthy results with your underwriter. Let's say if you would bring your boss a box of Chocolate on a bad day. This cover letter with little notes might be able to move your files quicker and more efficiently in the long run. I'm not an underwriter, but I would venture to say anything that would make my work world run smoothly, would greatly be appreciated.

Think about it- Put yourself in the underwriter's shoes for a moment each time you are preparing a loan file to submit. How long will take the underwriter to sort through what they are about to receive in your file? How long will it take them to determine the borrower's, the lender, the loan type, the property type, the loan purpose, the credit score and other relevant details?

**Here's an example** of cover letter or an overview of details that can make a workday of difference to an underwriter:

Borrower: New Homeowner (borrower's name)
Loan Type: Conventional Purchase with MI LTV/CLTV: 95/95
Property Type: Single Family home
Credit: Credit Scores 728/745/732
AUS: DU Approve/Eligible DTI: 24/36

Borrower: Mr. Borrower (borrower's name) is a permanent resident.
He has been in the working for same employer for nearly 6 years. Mr. Borrower (name) is a first-time homebuyer and is anxious about taking possession.

Credit: Mr. Borrower has minimal credit established, but all his bills have been paid in a timely manner, with the exception of one student loan that reflects a past due payment. The borrower also has an outstanding medical collection in which he has a written explanation, see enclosed document for written explanation.
Employment: Stable employed, same employer past 6 years. Used annual salary divided by 12 months + 24 month average of bonus earnings to qualify. Full VOE along with a current pay stub and IRS tax transcripts for last year are included.

**Assets:** Source of down payment is checking, savings and a withdrawal from 401-k account. Documentation of the vested account balance and loan terms is included in the submission. Mr. Borrower is waiting for income tax return check to come in the mail. As soon as it arrives, he will provide a copy of the check and deposit receipt from his bank and I will forward to underwriting. Note: that with all verified assets, Mr. Borrower will have about four months of reserves remaining in his account after closing.

**Debts/Liabilities:** The only debts Mr. Borrower will have in addition to the subject PITI are his car loan, and student loan payments. He pays his credit card balances off monthly. I have included documentation showing such in the file.
Property: Mr. Borrower is purchasing a single family dwelling downtown LA. Because interior is not covered by his master policy, I made the new owner aware that he will need to obtain and present evidence of insurance coverage. He is in the process of checking around with agents and will forward the policy information within the week. I will submit the evidence as soon as I receive it from him. I have compared the appraisal information with Fannie Mae's guidelines and it appears to meet requirements.

**Processing - Verification - Packaging**
**Important Needed Documents**
At various points during the loan process, lending will require documents related to the borrowers, and the property in which they are seeking a mortgage loan. At this point in the file process, all documentation should be collected, analyzed and entered into the database. The borrowers should have already provided copies of all-important documentation that is needed for their loan. The borrower's loan file should include a copy of their accepted offer on the property being purchased, and the executed sale agreement. The appraisal and title should have already been ordered/requested and received. The only thing left to do is pack it up and submit it to the underwriter/lender.

Once the loan is packaged and submitted to the lender or underwriting; they should respond within 48 hours with an approval or loan denied. If the borrower's credit is good, and they have a steady substantial income the loan should be approved. Though, it's not uncommon for underwriting to request further conditions from the borrowers on the loan. This is referred to as, underwriting conditions.   Usually, the underwriter presents conditions closer to the beginning of the loan, so they can be collected right away. However, underwriting and the lender monitor the borrower's loan up to the last signature on the document.

**Underwriting Conditions:** Sometimes the automated underwriting process, or the underwriter feels it is necessary to get additional information to make a decision on the loan. In this case, as soon as your mortgage banker lets you know that there are conditions to clear, get the information or take care of the tasks immediately. This is when most loans can be delayed because of the time it takes most companies to get the information to you.

**Why more underwriting conditions?**   Something in the borrower's loan may have changed between the times of application to closing? The borrowers could have gone on a shopping spree? The borrower's property they are purchasing my not had appraised for full value? There are several issues that could cause the loan to be delayed or possibly be denied. It is extremely important the borrowers understand the lender will monitor their file to the final closing. Remind the borrowers, they should not go on a shopping spree or change their status in any way before closing.
When all of the conditions are cleared, the lender or title company will issues a "clear to close" and the closing may be scheduled a few days later. Closing cannot be scheduled until all of the conditions are cleared.

If denied, the prospective borrower should talk to the lender in order to devise a plan and find out why the application was denied. By law, the prospective borrower should receive a disclosure statement from the lender in writing that states why the application was turned down.

**Ok, let's get this loan file to underwriting and close.**

**Stacking Order- Before file is submitted to underwriting-**
IF you need help in the beginning, please ask the LO or another processor.  They will be happy to assist you.  A basic outlined guideline used for a complete loan package, including borrower documentation and verifications.

The file content should be placed in an exact, particular order when submitted to the lender/underwriter.  The lender's underwriter reviews the documents in the order that is unique to that company, firm or individual investor. Each loan type has separate criteria, and each lender may use distinct file formats. The processor needs to know and will learn the order.

**Basic Stacking Order**

Imagine yourself as the underwriter attempting to fit several loans in your workday, everyday. Imagine receiving bits and pieces of information from various sources without any organization or order whatsoever. Imagine you trying to make sense out of pages of information and loose documents in a timed manner. It would be next to impossible. That is why an organized stacking order is most important to everyone involved in the mortgage loan process. Furthermore, think of it from the borrower's perspective, organization can help to make the loan signing go smoothly and more quickly. Most mortgage companies consider the following stacking order easier for the borrowers for signing and submitting documents. It's recommended to organize the borrower's package in such a way that the lender or underwriter can see the main terms within the first few documents. This is not only the key information they want to see but will generally be the point where any questions or issues will come up.

**Example:** If the note is toward the end of the package, and the interest rate is not acceptable to the borrower a lot of time has just been spent reviewing and signing for nothing. It may help to think of the stacking order like a shopping list? We may go shopping for many items, but there are certain things we do not want to forget. The lender/underwriter will want to see any key notes, the loan terms, requested loan amount, the credit worthiness of the borrowers and most of all; they will want to see who the borrowers are.

**These Legal Forms are also known as number-**
1003 (loan application)
1004 (appraisal)
1005 (VOE-Verification of Employment)
1006 (VOD-Verification of Deposit)

**List of documents, disclosures, and verifications the processor should have in a loan file.**

It might be beneficial for you to print this stacking order list and check off and date each document requested and received?

**File order**
File Loan Compliance documents

**HUD-1 Settlement Statement** must be signed and included in the document package

**Legal forms:**
FNMA 1003 (loan application)
FNMA 1004 (appraisal)
FNMA 1005 (VOE-Verification of Employment)
FNMA 1006 (VOD-Verification of Deposit)
HUD/RESPA good faith estimates GFE

**Verifications**
Personal identification
Employment and income verification (VOE)
1099's or W 2's
Self employment for 2 years include tax returns
Last two pay stubs
Sources for wages, salary, pension, commission
Bank verification (VOD)
Checking and savings accounts
Past 3 months bank statements
Credit union, retirement fund & investment accounts

**Address verification: landlord or lender**
Credit verification:
from independent reporting company
Debts including student loans
May use 3 month's utility bills

**Property verification:** rental agreements & appraisal report with appraiser signature
Disposition of work requirements by review appraiser and Association data (CC&R's)

**Disclosures**:
Lead-based paint, earthquake
Equal Opportunity (ECOA) notice
Adjustable interest rate (ARM) disclosure
Mortgage insurance (MIP) letter
FHA/VA assumption letter
Loan servicing agreement

**Title Document Clearance**
Disposition of liens
Documentation of bankruptcy, divorce, judgments
Preliminary Title Commitment - Title report

**Loan Package**
Credit report and data, gift letter, child support
Cover letter & transmittal summary
Underwriting guidelines & quality control
Association information **if applicable**
Broker fee
Rental agreements & Purchase agreement
Work completion and pest control

**Insurance-**

Flood insurance
Hazard insurance

**Military Income if applicable**
Commission Income
Overtime & Bonus Income
Part-time or Second-job Income
Retirement Income
Social Security Income
Alimony or Child Support
Notes Receivable
Interest Income & Dividends

**Net Rental Income**
GSI Gross scheduled income
Vac/BD Vacancy & bad debt
EGI Effective gross income
OE Operating Expenses (TIMMUR)*
NOI Net operating income
Mortgage Loan Brokering & Lending
OE = T Taxes (property) I Insurance (property, flood, earthquake) M Maintenance & repairs M Management (property) U Utilities R Reserves for replacement

**IRS Form 4506-T**
Request for Transcript of Tax Return
Transmitted for fax or mail
1040 and W-2 information
Attachments for various schedules
Instructions if copy must be certified for court or administrative proceeding

**Borrower Self Employed Documentation** if applicable
Self-Employment
Minimum two years (24 months) documented income
Copy of business card
Copy of business license
Bank statements for the past six months
Quarterly tax estimates payment records
Profit & Loss (P&L)
**Gift letter**

Undisclosed debt written explanation
Revolving debt: 5% of outstanding balance
Judgments, garnishments or Liens

**Bankruptcy If applicable**
Cosigned
Student loans
Cosigner documentation

**For cash out, include a statement of loan purpose**
Lane Guide
Provides correct lender mailing address☐ for:
Re-conveyance deed, payoff quotes and documents
Assignee & Assumption
Payoff documents
Foreclosure documents & REO
Fax, 800 numbers and email contact
Wholesale lending
Account rating and verifications of deposit
Rates and fees, hours & location of loan accounts

It's possible any or all of the above documents could be enclosed; this would depend upon each borrower's loan condition. There is no way of knowing exactly which documents are needed because each loan varies in degree.

**Help Tip:** In each borrower's loan file, there are probably 35-60 documents and disclosures. There is no way or need to memorize all of these forms, documents and disclosures. In the following list, not all documentations will apply to every loan. The loan officer or lender will advise you which documents are needed. You will learn more about all of these forms the longer you are with the mortgage industry. You can also do further investigation anytime online to better your knowledge.

**Submit or entering a loan to Desktop Underwriter (DU) for underwriting**
The first step, below, assumes that you are in the Quick 1003 for the loan you want to submit. (1003 Borrower's Loan Application)

Step 1. When you have completed all of the sections of the 1003 (borrower's loan application) that are required for underwriting, scroll to the bottom of any 1003 section and click Submit.

Step 2. The Select Credit and Underwriting Options screen appears. In the list box, click Underwriting Only, and then click next.

3. If required data is missing or incorrect, an error message appears. To correct the problem, click the link for the missing or incorrect data in the error message. You return to the section in the 1003 where the problem occurred.
Tip: If the loan contains numerous errors, you can print a copy of the error message so that you can correct all of the errors before you resubmit the loan for underwriting. To print the error message screen, select Print from your browser's File menu.    When the last error has been corrected, click Submit.

Step 4.  If you needed to correct errors in the 1003, the Select Credit and Underwriting Options screen appears again when you click Submit. In the list box in this screen, click Underwriting Only, then click Next.

Step 5. The Select an Underwriting Service screen appears. Select Desktop Underwriter, and then click Submit.

Step 6. A processing screen appears indicating the status of your request. Simply wait for the processing to complete.

Step 7. When the processing screen is complete, the Loan Information screen displays the status of your underwriting request. When the underwriting findings become available, the underwriting recommendation appears as a link under Underwriting Recommendation.

You can click the link for the recommendation to view the Underwriting Findings report and the Underwriting Analysis report. You can also click the View Findings link in the navigation bar of the Loan Information screen.

 Quick 1003 - is assuming you have already ordered or reissued a credit report.

Need additional help?  **See how to section for basic help – detailed help available on the Freddie Mac website.**  Desktop Underwriting DU and LP

https://www.fanniemae.com/content/job_aid/du-loan-underwriting-recommendation.pdf

**The red flags that underwriters are trained to look for-**
No processor wants to get clobbered with mountains of underwriting conditions? Therefore, be careful not to lose or fail to request and receive any needed documentation. Careful not to misspell or transpose any information and verify all phone numbers and address as well as an email address.

**Incomplete Application 1003- Check** all borrowers and co-borrower's information and make sure that every section of the loan application is fully and accurately completed. Double-check the spelling of your borrower's name.

• **Un-Reviewed Tax Returns**– Look for un-reimbursed business expenses, correct income information, marital status, clarifications, etc.

• Illegible faxes – Make sure all copies and scans are clear, and send new copies promptly when needed.

• **Un-Reviewed Bank Statements**– Always look for large deposits, overdrafts, negative balances, missing pages, and any other red flags. Be proactive about sending LOE's as needed. If you need clarification on something, then you know the underwriter will too. Get an LOE from the borrower and include it with your submission.

• **Incorrect GFE's**– Lender/Borrower credit, dates, and COC's need to be accurate on the initial, final and any re-disclosed GFE's.

• **Unrealistic Expectations of Timing**– Save your rush requests for true rush files. Work with your loan officer to establish an appropriate turn around time.

If a loan receives a "clear-to-close" earlier than expected, allow time for all departments to do their jobs in order to close the loan successfully. Remember, same-day and next-day closings are stressful on everyone and leave more room for errors.

• **Disclosing Incorrectly** – Make sure that the borrower and the loan officer have signed and dated all disclosures as applicable. Always re-disclose your TIL, GFE, and COC's when there is a loan amount change, program change, rate change, or rate lock.

• **Errors When Pulling Credit** – double check the spelling of your borrower's name and their social security number when pulling credit reports. Errors can cause additional reports to be pulled and possible loan declines. Remember to consider the non-purchasing spouse's credit and debt when applicable.

Make sure to include the title insurance and other closing costs documentation.

WRITE IT DOWN NOW!!
• Borrower's Communication – Discuss conditions submitted with the borrower before submitting to underwriting. Be proactive in your communications with your borrower. Take advantage of borrower questions and communications to build relationships with your borrowers. Talk to your borrower about why their file was declined or suspended. Return calls and emails.

**Sample Borrower's Conversation sheet**
Borrower: _____ Loan #: _____

Date_____

Spoke With Remarks Employee's Name
_____

Any information that has any bearing on the loan, the property, or the borrower should be written down here. Whether it is a phone call, information received through other channels, or just knowledge or speculations.

**Loan Officer's Communication-**
**Conversation sheet**

Loan Officer: _____ Borrower's Loan #: _____
Date _____

Spoke With and Remarks   Name
_____

Lender's Communication-
**Lender's Conversation sheet**
Lender : _____ Borrower's Loan #: _____

Date _____

Spoke With and Remarks   Name
_____

**Quick recap** - The loan officer works with borrower to complete the application process. The loan officer collects a number of supporting documentation from the borrowers and puts them in order. The loan officer foresees any unusual circumstances that may affect the borrower's loan approval. If any concerns should appear, he or she will work with the borrowers to get this corrected if possible. The loan office writes a cover letter to the lender that emphasizes the strong points and "sells" the lender and underwriter on a borrower.

The loan officer compiles the borrower's documentation, including any specific notes, and then passes the file to the loan processor for completion. The processor will order the title and appraisal along with any additional information the lender may need. This may include, for instance, verification of borrower's bank balances, employment, and mortgage or rental payment history, etc...

The processor will continue to collect and processes the rest of the required documents needed before the lender can guarantee funding. When and if the **lender, not loan officer** gives final approval on the borrower's loan, the borrower can then close the deal and take possession of their financed property. This cannot take place until the borrowers meet all the lending guidelines and satisfy all loan conditions. This is the point in the process that all parties involved must work together in a timely manner.

**Please see resources and forms for more reference if needed.**

**Tip:** We have included an awesome mortgage glossary in this training guide. We highly recommend reading and familiarizing yourself with the mortgage terms. This will help you have a better understand of the different forms, and what they represent.

# Chapter Five

## The Loan Closing

### Step Five: The loan closing

Closing (or settlement) is the legal process of transferring ownership of a home from one person to another. Two issues can make closing seem complicated — the number of documents and the costs involved

### Mortgage Processor or Senior Mortgage Processor- Depending on company and experience –

1, Basic duties directly associated with the loan closing. Communicate directly with all members to obtain the information and/or documentation necessary to make a loan decision.

2, Perform a full range of mortgage loan processing steps to accept an originated loan application and accurately complete all steps to ensure the loan package is fully prepared for closing. Prepare loan closing documentation; coordinate closing schedules with the Loan Closing Specialist; utilize checklists to ensure all essential documentation will be available at the closing.

3, Prepare loan closing documentation; coordinate closing schedules with the Loan Closing Specialist; utilize checklists to ensure all essential documentation will be available at the closing. It's very helpful to utilize a checklist to organize, request and prepare all essential documentation for the mortgage loan file from processing to closing.

The loan processor should have ordered and review credit reports, reviewed content for inclusion and accuracy, including: signed and dated **application**, **general authorization**, **rate lock** and **servicing disclosure**, wage and tax information, financial statements, legal documents such as divorce decrees and child support, construction documents; **flood certificate**, **HMDA** (home mortgage disclosure act) and other necessary or pertinent documentation. The processor should have verified that required information has been mailed, including the "**Truth in Lending**" and disclosure and other necessary documents; review all documents for compliance and make necessary corrections, track documentation until applications are complete.

Processor or lender should have ordered **flood certifications**, **appraisals** (checked to make certain of the correct type and location) and tracked for timeliness. Notified the member if the **property flood zoning** is questionable. Processor should have already reviewed and signed off on appraisals when received, enter pertinent information and process the appraisal bill.

The processor should have already packaged up the borrower's file and submitted to underwriting to prepare for closing.

This is like preparing to board an airplane. You try to find a travel deal to your designated location and purchase your airline ticket. You use a checklist to pack your needed garments as well as other important items. If you are traveling to the ocean on vacation, you really don't want to forget your swimsuit or sunscreen. If you do, it's to the store to purchase the items again. This error or lack of organization cost you extra time and money.

**Key elements of a closing**
As soon as the borrower receives a firm loan approval from the lender the actual closing date should be scheduled or confirmed. The estimated closing date was probably specified under the sale contract, but the lender or other mortgage specialist must set an actual close date. The borrowers want to make sure that settlement will take place before their loan commitment expires and before any rate lock agreement (guaranteed terms of the loan) expires. The settlement date also has to allow adequate time to assemble all of the required documentation. If repairs or maintenance on the property are a part of the lender's commitment, there must be time to complete them.

The real estate agents involved in the sale transaction and the lender are often the best people to coordinate the closing arrangements. Most lenders require at least 3 to 5 days advance notice of the closing date in order to prepare the loan documents and get them to the closing agent Within 24 hours prior to the actual closing, the borrower's real estate agent should make a final inspection of the property. This inspection is to make sure any required repairs have been completed, and the property is as described as the sale contract. The inspection usually includes everything that was written in the contract such as the kitchen appliances, carpeting and drapery. The inspector also checks that no recent fire or storm damage has occurred. In some cases, the lender will make a similar inspection before closing.

**When the borrower's loan file is complete-**
The lender or underwriting department will review all the documentation and decide whether to approve or deny it. If approved, the last step in the process is the closing meeting, in which the borrowers sign all the closing documentation. These are additional forms and documents the borrowers will sign at closing. These documents are not to be confused with the files in your file. The borrowers can then take possession of their property once their loan is completely closed.

**The event:**
There are two types of closings. One type brings all the parties together at a closing table. The other allows the parties to execute the documents separately through an escrow process. For purposes of illustration, we'll focus on the type where all the parties assemble together. In most cases, a "closing agent" conducts closing. This person may work for the lender or the title company or may be an attorney representing borrowers or their lender. He or she knows what documents need to be reviewed and will have collected all the necessary paperwork from the borrowers, the seller and the lender.

Several things happen here:
- Terms of the agreement between the borrowers and the mortgage lender are confirmed.
- Borrower's loan goes into effect and they receive their mortgage
- What the borrowers and the seller agreed to in the sales contract is confirmed.
- Ownership of the home is transferred.

Each of these steps normally involves several legal documents, each with costs for research and preparation. That's why there were so many documents compiled to review, sign and pay for at the closing and why some states require the borrowers to have an attorney present.

**Who attends?**
This can vary, but the closing agent and the borrowers or someone representing the borrowers is always present.
The seller, or someone representing him or her, is usually present, too, and real estate professionals (loan officer and lender) for them and the seller may or may not attend. A representative of the lender also may attend.
The closing agent makes sure everything is signed and recorded and that the funds collected for various fees and expenses are properly disbursed. The agent will explain each document and give the borrowers and their attorney (if in attendance) the chance to look at them. There are a lot of documents.

**Scheduling the closing:**
As stated earlier, as soon as the borrowers receive final loan approval, they should confirm the time and date of settlement with the seller and the lending. Usually, the real estate agents representing the borrowers and the seller are in the best position to coordinate the closing.
If the borrowers are scheduling their closing themselves, keep the following points in mind:

- They should allow enough time to complete all required documents
- They should allow time for any required repairs or maintenance on the house to be completed
- They should schedule before their loan commitment expires
- They should schedule before any rate lock agreement on their loan expires.
- Just before the scheduled closing within 24 hours -they should plan time to make a final inspection of their new home with their real estate professional, ensuring that no recent damage has occurred and that the seller has honored all repair agreements

**What the borrowers need to bring to closing:**
The closing agent will generally be responsible for preparing or ordering all the documents for their closing. However, they are responsible for the following, which they must bring to their closing:

The borrower's new homeowner's insurance policy and any other required insurance policies they have taken out, along with proof of payment. In most cases the processor or lender will require a review of the homeowner's insurance policy and proof of payment prior to scheduling the closing.

The borrowers must bring a certified check for all closing costs, including the remaining portion of their down payment. They will receive this figure a day or two before their closing from the closing agent. The borrowers are entitled to a copy of the **HUD-1 Settlement Statement** a minimum of 24 hours prior to the closing of the loan. This statement itemizes the services provided and fees charged to them. These fees should be negotiated prior to the closing.

**Closing costs, fees, and taxes:**
The fees listed here are typically associated with settlements throughout the country. As noted above, the borrowers should have received an estimate of their anticipated closing costs from you or the lender shortly after they applied for their mortgage. The borrower can get an exact figure for all final costs a day or two before their closing from the closing agent.

**Application fee:**
Often charged when the borrowers complete their mortgage application, this covers the lender's initial costs to process their application. In some cases, the application fee includes the cost of the property appraisal and credit report. The borrowers may want to confirm with the lender if these fees are included or are being charged as separate fees.

**Appraisal fee:**

This fee may also be charged when the borrowers complete their application. It covers the costs of an independent appraisal of the value of the home they're planning to buy for the lender's use in evaluating their application. The borrowers may be asked to pay for their credit report at the same time they pay for the appraisal. In some cases, they may be instructed to pay the fee to the property appraiser when this person arrives to perform the property appraisal.

**Loan origination fee:**
This fee covers remaining costs associated with processing your mortgage application and completing their loan. This fee is usually expressed and charged as a percentage of the loan amount.

**Discount points:**
Discount points are finance charges paid when they close on their loan usually to obtain a mortgage with a lower interest rate. Usually, a lender will offer a number of mortgages with different combinations of interest rates and discount points; the higher the interest rate, the fewer the discount points charged at closing. Discount points are charged as a percentage of the loan amount. One point is 1 percent of the value of the mortgage (for example, $800 on an $80,000 mortgage). Points are paid to the lender.

**Transfer taxes:**
Local governments generally charge transfer, recordation and property taxes when a home changes ownership. In some parts of the country, these taxes can be substantial. The borrowers cannot reduce them, but they may be able to negotiate with the seller to share them when they make their offer. However, some states require either the seller or the buyer to pay these or require they be split between the two parties. These are not paid to the lender but directly to the government entity at closing.

**Title: insurance:**
In most states, the government does not determine ownership of property. Changes in ownership are recorded at the local government level, and "title searches" are necessary to trace ownership. For this reason, most lenders require that borrowers purchase **title insurance** to cover the lender in the event there is a claim on the property that is not known at the time of closing. In addition, although it is not required, most buyers also purchase title insurance for themselves. It covers legal costs in the event of a future claim on the property.

Although home buyers can choose their own title insurance, most simply allow the real estate professional or the lender to choose it for them. Recent events, however, suggest that owners may want to be more directly involved in choosing the title insurance issuer.

The U.S. General Accounting Office (GAO) issued a report in April 2007 suggesting that title insurance may be priced higher than necessary.

**Other fees:**

The borrowers may have other fees or costs at their closing as well. If they are assuming the seller's mortgage, for example, there may be an assumption fee. The amount is set by the lender but could vary between several hundred dollars and one percent of the loan. The borrowers and the seller may have negotiated other payments that will be settled at the closing, such as prorated payments for condominium fees or property taxes. They also may have to pay for the services of the closing agent in conducting the closing.

**Documents they will receive**

Here are some of closing documents they should receive.

**Settlement Statement — HUD-1 Form:**

Prepared by the closing agent, this form lists all the important details regarding the sale/purchase of their new home: price, amount of financing, loan fees and charges, prorated real estate taxes and amounts paid between the buyer (borrower) and the seller. Both borrowers and the seller must sign it. The lender will keep the original.

**Documents at Closing:**

The following documents are typically required for closing:

There are standard documents and exhibits that are commonly required for a loan closing, regardless of jurisdiction. Some of these will be your responsibility, some the lenders and loan officer and others will be the responsibility of the seller.

- ID Sheets/Patriot Act Identification Form
- ID/Name Affidavit
- HUD-1 Settlement Statement
- How to receive proceeds (if it's in the package)
- Good Faith Estimate GFE (if it's in the package)
- Note
- Any riders to note
- Automatic payment form (if it's in the package)
- Initial Escrow Account Disclosure Statement
- First Payment Due Letter
- First Payment letter
- Truth in Lending
- Itemization of Amount Financed
- Mortgage/DOT
- Any riders to Mortgage/DOT

- RTC Beyond this, the order is not that important
- Payoff Authorization Letter
- Oral Agreement Disclosure
- Privacy Policy
- Impound Account Authorization
- Servicing Transfer Disclosure
- Borrowers Certification and Authorization
- Signature Name Affidavit
- Hazard Insurance Authorization and Requirements
- Notice of Required Flood Insurance
- Errors and Omission/Compliance Agreement
- Limited Power of Attorney
- Compliance Agreement
- Title docs such as Survey Affidavit, Owner's Affidavit, Affidavit & Indemnity, Occupancy Affidavit, etc
- Other items such as:
  1003 (Uniform Residential Loan Application)
  W-9
  4506-T
  4506
- Closing Instructions

All other items

**Section Terms:**

**The Title Company** typically prepares the following documents for the closing; deed, legal description, buyer and seller affidavits, and any other documents pertaining to the issuance of title insurance. Depending on the lender, they may also prepare some or all of the following; mortgages, notes, 1st payment letters, escrow docs etc.

**The Lender's package** will typically include the closing instructions, so the title company can prepare the settlement statement, and the mortgage, note, escrow analysis, 1st payment letter, etc. Depending on the lender, receipt of closing package can be anywhere from three days to one hour before the closing.

**Truth in Lending Act (TILA)**
Shortly after the borrowers applied for their mortgage, they received a truth-in-lending statement from the lender, including their estimated monthly payment and the total cost of all finance charges involved in their mortgage. They'll get a final TILA statement at the closing if these amounts have changed.

**Mortgage note:**
The mortgage note is legal evidence of their mortgage and includes their formal promise to repay the debt. It also spells out the amount and terms of the loan, along with the penalties the lender can impose if they do not make their payments on time as well as any prepayment penalties that may be required.

**Deed of trust:**
This document gives the lender a claim against the house if they don't live up to the terms of the mortgage. It lists the legal rights and obligations of the borrowers and the lender, including the lender's right to foreclose on the home if they default on the loan.

**Settlement Statement** - The settlement statement is prepared by the title company prior to the closing and is basically just a compilation of all the above information. Preparation time can vary from 1 to three hours given the complexity of the transfer and accuracy of the documentation. The following items must be addressed:
a. Consideration and prepayment to seller
• Purchase price
• Prepaid items such as; taxes, rent, utilities, homeowner's fees.
b. Credits to Buyer such as; earnest money, mortgage amount, prepaid rents and/or security deposits, seller paid closing costs, etc.

**Title Insurance Policy:** Every lender will require title insurance. The preferred company issuing the title insurance policy will have researched legal records to make sure that the borrowers are receiving clear title, or ownership, to the property. Their title search has established that the seller of the property is the legal owner, and that there are no claims, or liens, against the property. The title company offers both a lender's policy and an owner's policy. They will have to pay for a lender's policy and it is advisable for them to have an owner's policy as well. For a small additional premium, it will protect them up to the full value of the property if fraud, a lien or faulty title is discovered after closing.

**The Good Faith Estimate and Disclosure Statement**
When borrower's application is approved, they will receive a good faith estimate (GFE). This is an estimate summary of all the settlement charges plus their monthly payments. Information related to their property taxes, and homeowner insurance will be included if those charges are to be paid out of an escrow account held by the lender. They also received a truth-in-lending disclosure statement. It shows them the total cost of their mortgage over the life of the loan and breaks down their interest rate and all the components of the monthly payment.

**Homeowner's Insurance:**
The lender will require the borrowers to have homeowners insurance on the property at least in the amount of the replacement cost of the property. They should make sure the policy covers the value of the property and contents in the event they are destroyed by fire or storm. They must pay for the policy and have it at closing. They are free to select the insurance carrier, but the lender will require the company to meet rating standards and be rated by a recognized insurance rating agency.

**Termite Inspection and Certification:**
In many areas of the country, the property must be inspected for termites and the inspection is required in the purchase contract. In some parts of the country, this may be called a "wood infestation" report. The report is required on all FHA and VA loans as well as many conventional loans.

**Survey or Plot Plan:**
The lender may require a survey of the property, showing the property boundaries, the location of the improvements, any easements for utilities or street right-of-way and any encroachments on the boundaries by fences or buildings. Encroachments can be minor, such as a fence, or may be serious and have to be corrected before closing. In some areas, an addendum to the title policy eliminates the need for a survey.

**Water and Sewer Certification:**
If the property is not served by public water and sewer facilities, the borrowers will need local government certification of the private water source and sanitary sewer facility.

Properties with well and septic water sources are usually governed by county codes and standards.

**Flood Insurance:**

If the lender or the appraiser determines that the property is located within a defined flood plain, they will want, and the lender will require, a flood insurance policy. The policy must remain in force for the life of the loan.

**Certificate of Occupancy or Building Code Compliance Letter:**

If the borrower's home is new construction, they will have to have a Certificate of Occupancy, usually from the city or county, before they can close the loan and move in. The builder will obtain the certificate from the appropriate authority. Many local governments require an inspection when a home is sold to see if the property conforms to local building codes. Code violations may require repairs or replacement of structural or mechanical elements. The responsibility for ordering the inspection and paying for any required repairs should be spelled out in the purchase contract.

# Chapter Six

## How to Section

What's inside this section?

- How to open wide the door of opporutnity.
- Tips and suggestions:
- About a loan processing position?
- Employment leads and tips-
- Loan Applicaton: Form 1003   Step-by-Step breakdown-
- How to order or request verification and other forms-
- Analyzing and preparing you file for underwriting-
- Basic DU Overview-
- How to order or request verification and other forms
- Understanding the Appraisal

# Chapter Six

## How to Section

**How to open wide the door of opporutnity.** Write a good resume and set up appointments with employers. As complicated as it seems, becoming a loan processor is not that hard. Most banks and credit unions as well as mortgage companies are always hiring and offer on the job training. Banks, Car Dealers and other loan companies usually advertise in the local newspaper or on line at job seeker websites. You should write a good resume, sounding professional and include any financial type work that you have done before. If you don't have any mortgage loan experience, make sure you express that you are a people person, self-motivated and willing to learn. Try to obtain an understanding of the institution you are applying for and the types of loans they carry.

Use all previous work experience and training to benefit you. Example, if you were a cashier for any store, you would qualify for a bank teller since it's money-related as well as customer service. If you were ever a data entry person, you already have one much-needed skill for being a loan processing- Data entry. Now add customer service to that skill along with working with numbers and database, and you are equally qualified and experienced.  Are you beginning to see the big picture? Pull every past and present experience, resources and abilities into your application and interview.  Training is experience like branches to a tree; it keeps growing and forming new ones all the time. When doing these things, and you'll have a career in no time.  As long as there are people, there will be loans.

**Loan Processor Job Interview – You can do it!**

## Chapter Six

## How to section: continued

**Tips and suggestions:**

Smile and let your contribution in life shine through your face-
Put on confidence, selling your knowledge and your ability, but by all means, avoid being pushy or arrogant. True character is on the inside, not just an outward show. Be happy and exuberant, but certainly not annoying.

**Confidence** is generally described as a state of being certain either that a hypothesis or prediction is correct or that a chosen course of action is the best or most effective. **Self-confidence** is having confidence in oneself. Confidence can be a self-fulfilling prophecy as those without it may fail or not try because they lack it and those with it may succeed because they have it rather than because of an innate ability. **Avoid Arrogance** - Arrogance is having unmerited confidence—believing something or someone is capable or correct when they are not.

Self-confidence does not necessarily imply 'self-belief' or a belief in one's ability to succeed. For instance, one may be inept at a particular sport or activity, but remain 'confident' in one's demeanor, simply because one does not place a great deal of emphasis on the outcome of the activity. When one does not dwell on negative consequences one can be more 'self-confident' because one is worrying far less about failure or the disapproval of others following potential failure. One is then more likely to focus on the actual situation, which means that enjoyment, and success in that situation is also more probable.

Belief in one's abilities to perform an activity comes through successful experience and may add to, or consolidate, a general sense of self-confidence.

Studies have also found a link between high levels of confidence and wages. Seemingly, those who self-report they were confident earlier in schooling, earned better wages and were promoted more quickly over the life course.

Being your best during a job interview will be much easier when you know what to expect. The process may begin with an online questionnaire designed to give the employer some insight into your skills and your personality. Then there is the in-person interview, which may be scheduled as a one-on-one or as a panel interview. The employer will focus on your prior experience or knowledge and your decision-making ability. Showing confidence in yourself will be one of your best assets. Have ten years experience in the industry, but lack personality and confidence will not get you hired. On the other hand, you can have a great deal of knowledge attached to a confidant personality, will likely get you hired. All the experience in the world cannot compensate for confidence and personality.

If you're eating a burger with a grossed out look about you, I'm certainly not going to want to try it. The same goes if you can't convince yourself you're qualified; you are never going to convince anyone else either.

Always remember this: I can do all things through Christ Jesus who strengthens me- Philippians 4:13

**Looking for answers to common questions about loan processing?**

We've placed the answers to a few that should satisfy you and your pursuit in becoming a mortgage loan processor? If you have other questions, just let us know.

**1. How do I become a loan processor?**

Begin by learning about the various tasks the loan processor and loan officer are required to do. Comparing these will enable you to determine which position fits your personality and lifestyle. Some additional research will help you to determine which position(s) you are already qualified for or aspire to have. You can gain more insight on the responsibilities at various levels on loan processing and becoming a loan processor by visiting our website as well as Fannie Mae and Freddie Mac. You'll find the skills and characteristics that are customary to have on various mortgage loan jobs. For salary information and current job openings, you can visit websites like Salary.com or Monster.com. Be sure to check both federal and state licensing requirements to make sure you're in compliance.

**Employment leads and tips-**

There are many positions in the banking and financial industries, such as a loan processor. Most employers are often willing to hire applicants with only a high school diploma or GED. This is especially true for positions with smaller financial institutions. Many employers are willing to provide on-the-job training to an employee who possesses a good deal of knowledgeable about the mortgage process. Comprehension, along with some basic required skills could be your foot in the mortgage industry? Our Loan Processing training will give you the basic skills and comprehension needed to apply for job openings. These employers will allow qualified candidates to complete their training on the job. Financial institutions may also hire loan processors from within the institution.

**What is the difference between an in-house mortgage loan processor and a contract mortgage loan processor?**

**An in-house processor** or home grown is someone who already works within the company. For example, a financial institution may promote a person working as a bank teller into a loan processor position. Typically, an employee of the company, they may be assigned a group of loan officers that they work with on a consistent basis. Processors are usually compensated with an hourly wage or a salary and not commissioned like the mortgage broker or banker. These are compensated with bonuses that are tied to the achievement of production goals.

**A contract loan processor** is considered to be an independent contractor (aka self-employed). Although they work closely with a lender, broker or banker, they also have the freedom to enter into contracts with others. A successful contract processing company could very easily have relationships with 20 companies that originate loans. A contract processor is usually compensated on a per file basis with the details spelled out via the terms of an annual contract. Many contract processors are required to be licensed as an originator or a mortgage broker to meet industry guidelines for the states that they conduct business in. Contract processors will also need access to the same business equipment and software that an in-house process does. Make sure to budget for the purchase, maintenance and repair of these items if you plan to go solo.

**Notes**

# Chapter Six
## How to Section: continued

**Step-by-step loan application**
**Loan Applicaton: Form 1003   Step-by-Step breakdown**

There are 10 sections in the mortgage loan application that are described in detail here. The loan officer will assist the borrowers with many sections of this document, especially as they relate to the type of mortgage and terms of the mortgage loan.

### Section I: Type of Mortgage and Terms of Loan

The information in this section should match the type of mortgage and mortgage loan terms that was discussed with the loan officer and borrowers. For purchases where they haven't selected a property yet, they can specify the maximum amount they wish to borrow.

### Section II: Property Information

If they've already selected a house, in this section they will need to provide information about the property, including the address, the year it was built, whether they want to purchase or refinance, as well as other details about the purpose of the mortgage loan they seek.

### Section III: Borrower Information

This is personal information required of all if any co-borrower involved (any additional borrower who accepts responsibility for paying the mortgage, such as their husband or wife), including Social Security number, date of birth, marital status, and contact information (street address and telephone numbers). If they have lived at their current address less than two years, they should be prepared to furnish former addresses for up to seven years.

With this identifying information, the lender will be able to obtain their credit report, which is a key factor in helping the loan officer assess their current financial situation.

### Section IV: Employment Information/
### Section V: Monthly Income and Combined Housing Expense Information

In these sections, the borrowers will need to provide a history of their employment (where they have worked and for how long), their monthly income, and their monthly expenses (bills they pay every month), along with recent paycheck stubs and federal W-2 income tax forms for the last two years. With this information, the loan officer can determine their ability to make regular payments on the mortgage and their capacity to afford the costs associated with owning a home. If they have not worked at their current job for at least two years, or if they have multiple jobs, they will need to provide information on all jobs going back until they have a two-year history. The loan officer will have them sign a Verification of Employment (VOE) form, which will be sent to their employer to verify their employment and earnings. A VOE form will also be sent to previous employers if they have been on the job less than two years. Use their gross income for the Monthly Income column in Section V. Their gross income is how much money they make before taxes or deductions. This includes most sources of income, although they aren't required to disclose alimony, child support or separate maintenance payments if they do not choose to have them considered for paying your mortgage.

The information they provide will later be verified by a credit report ordered by the loan officer or lender. Differences between their figures and those on the credit report will raise questions and may delay the decision on their mortgage loan, so it is important that they are as accurate as possible when filling out this section.

## Section VI: Assets and Liabilities

This section indicates the borrowers current financial position - how much they own (assets) versus how much they owe (liabilities). The difference between the two is their net worth. If they have bank accounts, savings, retirement funds, investments, cars or trucks — even cash that they keep at home — they can be considered assets that support the application. They will need to provide copies of all of their account statements for at least two months.

For the Liabilities section, they will be asked to itemize all of their current bills, loans and other debts, including current balances and monthly payments. Debts include automobile loans, credit cards, finance company loans, bank and credit union loans and existing mortgages, including home equity loans.

The assets and liabilities information they provide to their loan officer on the loan application will later be verified by a credit report ordered by the loan officer or lender. If they have not yet established a credit record by obtaining a credit card or an auto loan, for example, the loan officer may look to see if they've paid their rent and utilities on time so they can evaluate their payment patterns.

## Section VII: Details of the Transaction
This section gives the all-important details of the mortgage loan - presented as estimates - including the purchase price of the home, closing costs, and the total cost of their mortgage loan (including principal, interest, and fees), among other information. The loan officer will complete this area of the application. Make sure that it agrees with their understanding of the transaction, looking closely at the estimated closing costs.

## Section VIII: Declarations

In this section, the borrowers will be asked to answer questions about any pending legal problems or other factors (past or present) that may influence their financial situation. For example, have they ever declared bankruptcy? This information, in combination with their credit report, will help the lender assess their ability to pay the mortgage. In addition, they will be asked to affirm if they are a U.S. citizen or a permanent resident alien. If they are not a U.S. citizen but can provide documentation to establish a legal presence in the U.S., they can still obtain a mortgage.

## Section IX: Acknowledgment and Agreement

The borrower's signature is their word of honor. In this section, they sign their name, saying that the information they are providing is accurate and true to the best of their knowledge.

## Section X: Information for Government

Monitoring Purposes In this section of the application, the borrowers will need to provide such information as their ethnic origin and their race. That's because the U.S. government wants to be sure our housing finance system meets the needs of every racial and ethnic group in the country. This is one way they gather the statistics they need to ensure the system works fairly for everyone.

## Notes

**Basic DU Overview**

**Setting up and ordering/requesting necessary documents**

When you first begin to use DU, an administrator in your company should setup the required tasks for the loan processes, and then you can perform the required tasks. **Help Tip:** We strongly suggest you follow our tip and get somewhat familiar with this program or software before interviewing. You can free, without any charge learn this program from the Fannie Mae website. Please try to research and learn the DU functions.

https://www.fanniemae.com/content/job_aid/du-wholesale-admin-guide.pdf

DU administrator login / set up (The loan officer and Loan processor)
The Loan List screen appears.

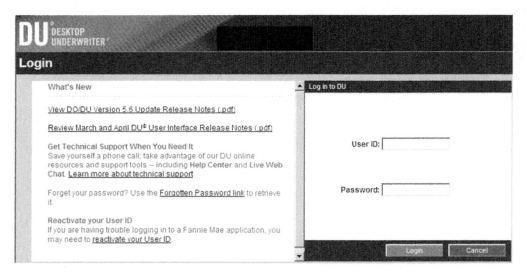

1. Enter your DU user ID and password, and then click Login. To access DU, you must have a valid user ID and password.
2. The Display Options screen appears. Select the application you want to work with (in this case, select Desktop Originator/Desktop Underwriter) and click choose an Application.
3. The Choose an Institution field appears. Choose your Institution.
4. The screen is refreshed listing the application and institution that you are accessing.

Using the Loan List –
DU maintains a record of all your loan case files for up to 270 days. Your case files are displayed in the Loan List, which has sort and search capabilities. You can look at all your loan case files, define a date range, or search for a specific case file. You can also sort the columns in the Loan List to display loan case files in an ascending or descending order.

**Sorting Loans**
You can sort the various columns in the Loan List to customize the display. Click a heading to determine how to sort the list. A down-facing arrow appears next to the heading that you selected, indicating the list is sorted in descending order. Select the heading again to sort the list in ascending order.

**Searching for Loans**
You can use the Loan Search area in the Loan List to locate and display a specific loan file or a set of files based on specified criteria. You can change the display as often as you wish.
If your organization has set up multiple institutions, you should begin your search for loan files by checking the name of the institution that appears in the Institution field at the top of the Loan Search area of the screen. If you need to search for loan files under a different institution, simply select that institution from the Institution field. To display recently modified loan files:

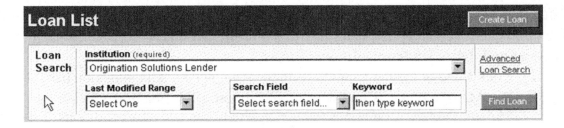

1. Click a date range in the Last Modified Range list to see files that you worked on in the past 1, 7, 30, 60, 90, 120, or 270 days.
2. Once you select a date range, click the Find Loan button.
3. To display loan files by Loan Number or by a borrower's last name, select an option in the Search Field (for example, Borrower Last Name), and then enter a keyword (for example, the last name of the borrower on the file you want to find). Once you select a search field and keyword, click the Find Loan button.

To search for specific loan files:
1. Click the Advanced Loan Search link.

The Advanced Loan Search screen appears with several options that you can use to search for the loan Files you want to view.

2. Enter the necessary information into each field that you want to use in the search. When you have finished with your selections, click the Search button. The following table describes each field and explains the data you will need to enter. Note that the more fields you select, the more restrictive your search will be.

- Institution: Using DU The Institution field is pre-filled for you.
- Loan number: Enter the Loan Number that your organization has assigned to the loan file you want to find. Be sure to enter it exactly as it appears in the loan data, including upper- and lower-case letters, spaces, and special characters.
- Casefile ID: Enter the unique casefile ID that DU assigned to the loan casefile when it was first created.

**Adding and Deleting Lender Conditions:**

You can establish default conditions that will be returned in the Fannie Mae Underwriting Findings report to all of your originators who submit loan file to you through DO. For example, you might want to inform originators that you require complete file receipt within 24 hours of a Final submission. With the Manage Lender Conditions function, you can add new lender conditions or delete existing lender conditions at any time.

Note: Lender conditions that you modify will apply only to loan file that are submitted after you add or delete the conditions.

**To add and delete lender conditions:**
1. Click Manage Lender Conditions in the Admin Tool left navigation bar.
2. The Manage Lender Conditions screen appears. The first time you use the Maintain Lender Conditions feature, you only can add new conditions. Type any conditions that you want to add to the Findings report in the Condition text boxes. When you are finished adding lender conditions, click Save Conditions.
   To modify a Lender Condition, make any changes in the applicable text box and click Save Conditions.
3. You return to the Loan List. After you add and save lender conditions, they will appear in the top part of the Maintain Lender Conditions screen the next time you access this function. To delete a condition, repeat steps 1 and When the Maintain Lender Conditions screen appears click the down arrow beside the condition you want to delete, then click Yes. When you have finished deleting conditions, click Continue.

**Releasing a Loan file to an Originator:**

When an originator performs a Final submission, control of the loan data is transferred to you, the lender. This means that the originator can no longer make changes to the loan file. However, there may be times when you want to return control of the file to the originator by releasing the loan file. Follow the steps below to release a loan file back to an originator.

Note: You can release a loan file regardless of whether the originator submitted it to you as an Interim or Final submission.

**To release a loan file:**
In the Loan List, locate the file you want to release, and click the Borrower name.
The Loan Information screen appears. In the navigation bar on the left side of the screen, click Release Loan.
The Release Loan screen appears. Review the information to be sure this is the correct loan file. To release the file, click the Release Loan button.
You return to the Loan List. Notice that the loan file you released no longer appears in the Loan List.

**Exiting from DU:**
To end your DU session and exit from the application, click the Log Out button located in the upper-right corner of the Loan List and Loan Information screens. A confirmation message appears. Click OK.

Recommended for you- Try using Fannie Mae's Help Center-
There is a robust online Help Center tool that you can access from every screen in DU. To access the Help Center, click the Help Center link in the upper left corner of any screen in DU.  https://desktopunderwriter.fanniemae.com

# Chapter six
## How to section: continued

### How to order or request verification and other forms

No book or training guide couold possibly contain all the information on how to do everything, however, Freddie Mac website has some great training resources that I am going to include here for you…

You must check this site out… I assure you, you will learn all there is to know about how to do all thes ordering and requesting functions.

If this link is not clickable, then please type web address into your web browser.

Basic DU overview http://www.freddiemac.com/singlefamily/underwrite/index.html

http://portal.hud.gov/hudportal/HUD?src=/program_offices/administration/hudclips/forms/hud9

https://www.fanniemae.com/singlefamily/selling-servicing-guide-forms

http://www.freddiemac.com/learn/uw/credit.html

http://www.freddiemac.com/sell/forms/index.html

https://www.fanniemae.com/singlefamily/selling-servicing-guide-forms

- Uniform Loan Application  1003
- Credit Report -
- Gift letter -
- Order Title-
- Order Aprasial -
- VOE – Verification of Employment
- VOD – Verification of Deposit
- VOM – Verification of Mortgage
- VOR – Verification of Rent
- VOD – Verification of Deposit

# How to section: continued

## What to do when you encounter underwriting problems

Assets Requirement for Underwriting

Assets are one of the essential conditions of underwriting. There are two major types of assets, liquid assets and non-liquid assets. Both are equally important when a file is underwritten, comparing with old times, where underwriters had to make final determination for the required assets, it is more easier nowadays when automated system makes all the determinations.

Most common assets include checking, savings, CD, Bonds, stocks and retirements accounts. Assets show stability for the borrower and gives confidence to the lending institution to grant more loans. It also provides a trend for the borrower's saving ability. Therefore, lenders know that in worse circumstances of employment instability, a borrower will be able to continue his mortgage payments.

## How to make sure your loan funds on time:

Borrower's file is now wrapped up, and your long and winding road to successfully processing their loan ends on the day of closing (also known as escrow closing, or settlement). You, the loan processor has sent the borrowers compete package to the lender/underwriter. The borrowers will go to the title company, or other designated place for closing to sign their mortgage documents, and transfers the home to their ownership. The lender and seller, or their representatives, and the real estate agents may or may not be at the actual closing. The actual loan closing procedure, including who conducts the closing and who is present, depends upon local laws and customs the lender practices. It is not unusual for the parties to the transaction to complete their roles without ever meeting face to face. The closing agent will make sure that all necessary papers are signed and recorded and that funds are properly disbursed and accounted for when the closing is completed.

## Understanding the Aprasial -Aprasial Report

### Appraising Collateral

A Real Estate appraiser appraises the borrower's property that he wishes to have the loan against. This is done to prevent fraud of any kind by either the borrower or the mortgage broker. This prevents fraud like "equity stripping" and money embezzlement. The amount that the appraiser from either the borrower's side or the lender's side is the amount that the borrower can loan up to. This amount is divided by the debt that the borrower wants to pay off plus other disbursements (i.e. cash-out, 1st mortgage, 2nd mortgage, etc.) and the appraised value (if a refinance) or purchase price (if a purchase) {which ever amount is lower} and converted into yet another ratio called the Loan to value (LTV) ratio. This ratio determines the type of loan and risk the lender is put up against. For example: if the borrower's house appraises for $415,000 and they wish to refinance for the amount of $373,500 - the LTV ratio would be 90%. The lender also may put a limit to how much the LTV can be - for example, if the borrower's credit is bad, the lender may limit the LTV that the borrower can loan. However, if the borrower's credit is in Good condition, then the lender will most likely not put a restriction on the borrower's LTV. LTV for loans may or may not exceed 100% depending on many factors.

The appraisal would take place on location of the borrower's property. The appraiser may take pictures of the house from many angles and will take notes on how the property looks. He/she will type up an appraisal and submit it to the lender or broker (depending on who ordered the appraisal.) The Appraisal is written in the format compliant to FNMA Form 1004. The 1004 is the standard appraisal form used by appraisers nationwide.

### Value: appraised, estimated, and actual

Since the value of the property is an important factor in understanding the risk of the loan, determining the value is a key factor in mortgage lending. The value may be determined in various ways, but the most common are:

Actual or transaction value: this is usually taken to be the purchase price of the property. If the property is not being purchased at the time of borrowing, this information may not be available.

**Appraised or surveyed value**: in most jurisdictions, some form of appraisal of the value by a licensed professional is common. There is often a requirement for the lender to obtain an official appraisal.

Estimated value: lenders or other parties may use their own internal estimates, particularly in jurisdictions where no official appraisal procedure exists, but also in some other circumstances.

Appraisal (ordered through an affiliated ordering team) – turn around time is usually 1-2 weeks. Two reports are required for loan amounts over 1 million

- Rent schedule (Investment properties only) – completed by the appraiser and turned in with the appraisal report.

- Title Policy (this request goes out to the Title Company) – Turn around times may vary depending on the Title Company and the subject property. Normally 2-5 days

- Insurance Policy (this request goes out to your Insurance Agent) Turn around times may very depending on your Insurance Agent. Normally 2-3 days

- Condo Approval (Condo units only, this request goes out to the Condo Association to complete) – There are usually cost involved with this request that are responsibility of the borrower. Turn around time depends on the Condo Association. Normally 3-5 days.

- Verification of Employment (VOE) (this request goes out to you employer to complete) – Turn around time depends on your Employer.

- Verification of Deposit (VOE) (this request goes out to your Bank to complete) – Turn around time depends on your Bank

- Social Security verification (this request is sent out to the Social Security Administration)  - Turn around time is 1-2 days

- 4506t Form (this request goes out to the IRS) Used to verify income. Turn around time is 2-3 days

- Fraud Guard (this is order through a computer system) – Turn around time is instantly

- Flood Certification (this is order through a computer system) – Turn around time is instantly
- Credit Report (this is requested through a computer system, normally at the begging of the process) – Turn around time is instantly
- Credit Supplements (this is requested through the credit agencies)
Used to bring any credit account up-to-date . Turn around time is 2-4 days

**Helpful tips and suggestions**

**Analyzing and preparing you file for underwriting**
More often than not, a denied loan file or one that experiences a significant delay in underwriting should have never been sent to the underwriter's desk. Having the skill to thoroughly evaluate a file and address potential issues early on is a must for quick turn-around time. In this section, you will learn what can be done during processing to eliminate delayed chaos.

**Underwriting Checkpoints: How to expedite your file with any lender**
What you need to know to shave days (maybe even weeks) off of your underwriting time? Here are some simple ways to expedite the loan process approval. Do not avoid phone calls and emails from anxious borrowers? Even better, your borrower will appreciate the great customer service you provided throughout the transaction.
Being precautionary in reviewing your files for errors before submission definitely makes your job easier in the long run. If your gut tells you "there's got to be a better way!" you're right, there is! Before submitting the file to underwriting, it is very important for a loan officer or processor to closely review the bank statements and address all deposits, which are unusual. On refinances, a borrower does not require funds for closing; therefore, in that case, providing explanation for any large and/or unusual deposits is good. If the transaction is a purchase then each deposit needs explanation and documentary proof for the deposit. If documentary proof is not available then that amount of assets is not used as verified assets for closing. If there is a deposit of a gift funds then a gift letter is required with donor's ability and a copy of the check.

**Here are a few of the questions that you should be prepared to answer in an interview for a loan-processing job.**

- Tell me about your most recent loan processing experience.
- What is/was your scope of authority (i.e., what type of decisions/activities were you allowed to make independently)?
- What origination/processing or automated underwriting systems are you proficient in?
- What are some of your favorite loan processing resources and why?
- What is the biggest challenge you have faced as a loan processor? How did you resolve that challenge?
- If there was one thing you could change about the way your current/most recent employer handles loan processing, what would it be and why?
- What support or resources do you feel you would need to make a smooth transition into our company?

- What is the highest number of files that you processed in a single month?
- What is the highest number of loan officers/agents you have worked with in a single month and what type of deals were in their pipeline?
- What lenders and third-party vendors have you worked with in the last 12 months?

Take classes or watch youtube.com to learn the following tasks. Learning these tasks will certainly open up more doors than you can ever imagine.
Learning any of these responsibilities on youtube is absolutely free and easy.
You can also learn everything you ever wanted or need to know from Fannie Mae and Freddie Mac websites as well as goggle search anything.

**Helping tip -** Watch and learn the entire list below and your opportunity will be boundless

- Read this book thoroughly before searching out a job.
- Know your stuff
- Be confident in yourself and your ability to perform the job.
- Have some personality – not timid or excessively bouncy
- Convince them to give your knowledge and abilities a chance.
- Try looking for loan processing jobs offering on-the-job training.
- Do lots of research on company before interviewing.
- Have a list of things you want to ask as well.
- Try all banks and Credit Unions
- Never lie, always be honest.
- Dress the part – no time to be slazzy-
- Make sure that the job is as perfect a match for you as it is for the employer.

**Never get discouraged and give up on anything in life.**

# Chapter six
## How to section: continued

**What is?**
**Underwriting Loan Conditions:**
Before a loan can be approved, it is going to have to go through an underwriting process. During the underwriting process, the underwriter is going to evaluate your application to determine if you are worthy of a loan. The underwriter may find something in the borrower's file that requires more information or documentation before deciding? They will then issue loan condition that states they want some type of additional information in order to process the loan. This could mean something as simple as missing information about the application, additional proof of income, certified copy of divorce, letter from the employer, something on the credit report needs to be discussed? It could be something simple to something to a major issue? An approval is a good thing, may just need some clarification on something.

**Liquid Assets**
Liquid assets can use us mean, if required right away. This category includes checking accounts, savings accounts, and gift funds and in some cases CD accounts. Normally, liquid assets are required for transactions where a borrower requires funds for closing. Liquid assets in a borrower's account need to be seasoned for, at least two months; otherwise an explanation is required with documentary proof for the large deposit. A borrower needs to prove that he/she has required funds for closing plus 2 to 6 month reserves (depending on the approval requirement) in his bank account. This requirement is sometimes satisfied through gift funds if a borrower is short in funds for closing. Gift funds can be used for closing but not for reserves. For reserves a borrower has to have their own funds, which could be non-liquid assets too.

**Non-Liquid Assets**
Examples for non-liquid assets are mutual funds, retirement, 401K, stocks and bonds. These assets can be used for both closing and reserves. If used for reserves, the borrower can only use 60% to 70% of the value. If the borrower does not have enough liquid funds for closing then he /she requires liquidation of these assets before the closing. Assets mentioned above can only be used if they can be liquidated. Underwriting cannot use these funds for reserves if the borrower is not able to liquidate these funds. Due to this reason, the underwriter has to always see the terms and conditions for liquidation. On the other hand, if a borrower is using his or her 401k for closing costs and/or down payment, then he or she is not required to provide terms and conditions for the liquidation of those accounts.

## Chapter Seven

**Chapter Seven**
Forms and Disclosures
National Component Pre-test  A-B-C
National Component Pre-test Answers
Glossary

## Credit Report - Understanding the Credit Report

### Decisions & credit risk

Depending if the borrower has credit worthiness, then he/she can be qualified for a loan. The norm qualifying FICO score is not a static number. Lender guidelines and mitigating factors determine this number. Not only does one's credit score affect their qualification; the fact of the matter also lies behind the question, "Can I (the borrower) afford this mortgage?" In most cases the borrower can afford their mortgage. However, some borrowers seek to incorporate their unsecured debt into their mortgage (secured debt.) They seek to pay off the debt that is outstanding in amount. These debts are called "liabilities," these liabilities are calculated into a ratio that lenders use to calculate risk. This ratio is called the "Debt-to-income ratio" (DTI). If the borrower has excessive debt that he/she wishes to pay off, and that ratio from those debts exceeds a limit of DTI, then the borrower has to either pay off a few debts in a later time or pay off just the outstanding debt. When the borrower refinances his/her loan, they can pay off the remainder of the debt.

Example: if the borrower owes $1,500 in credit cards and makes $3,000 in a month: his DTI ratio would be - 50%. But if the borrower owes $1,500 and makes $2,000 in a month, his DTI ratio would be - 75%. This ratio is seen by many lenders as high and too risky a person to lend to and may or may not be able to afford the mortgage. So that covers qualification, now on to appraising collateral.
Pricing, including Risk-based pricing & Relationship based pricing
Pricing policy varies a great deal. While you probably can't influence the pricing policy of a given financial institution, the borrower can:

- Shop around
- Ask for a better rate - some financial institutions will respond to this, some won't
- Price match - many financial institutions will match a rate for a current customer
Pricing is often done in one of these ways. Follow the internal links for more details:

- **Everyone pays the same rate.** This is an older approach, and most financial institutions no longer use this approach because it causes low risk customers to pay a higher than market rate, while high risk customers get a better rate than they might otherwise get, causing the financial institution to get a lower rate of return on the loan than the risk might imply.

- **Risk-based pricing.** With this approach, pricing is based on various risk factors including loan to value, credit score, loan term (expected length, usually in months)
- **Relationship based pricing** is often used to offer a slightly better rate to customers that have a substantial business relationship with the financial institution. This is often a price improvement offered on top of the otherwise computed rate.

**Credit bureau-**

**A credit bureau** or **consumer-reporting agency** (United States), or **credit reference agency** (United Kingdom) is a company that collects information from various sources and provides consumer credit information on individual consumers for a variety of uses. It is an organization providing information on individuals' borrowing and bill-paying habits. Credit information such as a person's previous loan performance is a powerful tool to predict his future behavior. Such credit information institutions reduce the effect of asymmetric information between borrowers and lenders, and alleviate problems of adverse selection and moral hazard. For example, adequate credit information could facilitate lenders in screening and monitoring borrowers as well as avoid giving loans to high-risk individuals. This helps lenders assess credit worthiness, the ability to pay back a loan, and can affect the interest rate and other terms of a loan. Interest rates are not the same for everyone, but instead can be based on risk-based pricing, a form of price discrimination based on the different expected risks of different borrowers, as set out in their credit rating.

Consumers with poor credit repayment histories or court adjudicated debt obligations like tax liens or bankruptcies will pay a higher annual interest rate than consumers who don't have these factors. Additionally, decision-makers in areas unrelated to consumer credit, including employment screening and underwriting of property and casualty insurance, increasingly depend on credit records, as studies have shown that such records have predictive value. At the same time, consumers also benefit from a good credit information system because it reduces the effect of credit monopoly from banks, and it provides incentives for borrowers to repay their loans on time.

## Chapter Seven: continuation
## Verification – Forms and Disclosures

Should you need additional help understanding any of these documents, see our how to section or resource section. If you cannot find the help in those two sections, please browse through Fannie Mae and Freddie Mac websites. They have an incredible learning website database for anyone to use for training or gaining mortgage knowledge.

**Note:** The documents here are for sample only- There is absolutely no way we could or want to include every document include in the loan process. It would be an entire book of forms and documents. We are not trying to train you on the documents themselves, but to process them.

Please refer to Fannie Mae or Freddie Mac as well as other websites offering free mortgage documents to train and view.

Initial Loan Application – 1003- 92900a

Turth in lending
Good Faith Estimate  GFE

ECOA – Equal Credit Opportunity Act-
Home Mortgage Disclosure
Preditory Lending
Usury
Rate Lock Confirmation -

Credit Report & Supporting Documentation
Income Documentation
60 days most recent bank statements
VOD – Veriffcation of deposit
W-2's two most recent years
paystubs documenting YTD earnings
VOE – Verificaton of employment
Lock Conformation
Verification of Assets
Earnest Money Deposit
Evidence of sufficient funds to close
Good Faith Estimate
Purchase agreement/Contract of Sale

Truth In Lending
Payoff Statement (Refinance Transactions)
ECOA, Fair Lending
FHA Appraisal report indicating the FHA case number on all pages
all applicable Addenda including FHA
Right To Receive an Appraisal
Conditional Commitment pages 1-6
Underwriting Checklist

Mandatory Disclosures
State Required Disclosures
Servicing Transfer Disclosure
FHA Assumption Policy Informed Consumer Choice Disclosure
Lead based paint disclosure
FHA DE Disclosure
Important Notice to the Homebuyer
For Your Protection Get A Home Inspection
Appraisal Logging Information
Additional Federally required Disclosures
Amendatory Clause and Real Estate Certification
Refinance Authorization for Streamline Transactions


Included in this section is several sample forms – Disclosures- Verifications-

Initial loan application below –
Uniform underwriting transmittal summary
Credit report
Gift letter
Disclosure of Information on Lead-Based Paint or Hazards

# Uniform Residential Loan Application

This application is designed to be completed by the applicant(s) with the Lender's assistance. Applicants should complete this form as "Borrower" or "Co-Borrower," as applicable. Co-Borrower information must also be provided (and the appropriate box checked) when ☐ the income or assets of a person other than the Borrower (including the Borrower's spouse) will be used as a basis for loan qualification or ☐ the income or assets of the Borrower's spouse or other person who has community property or similar rights pursuant to applicable state law will not be used as a basis for loan qualification, but his or her liabilities must be considered because the spouse or other person who has community property or similar rights and the Borrower resides in a community property state, the security property is located in a community property state, or the Borrower is relying on other property located in a community property state as a basis for repayment of the loan.

If this is an application for joint credit, Borrower and Co-Borrower each agree that we intend to apply for joint credit (sign below):

_____          _____

Borrower                           Co-Borrower

| I. TYPE OF MORTGAGE AND TERMS OF LOAN | | | | |
|---|---|---|---|---|
| **Mortgage Applied for:** | ☐ VA  ☐ USDA/Rural Housing Service ☐ FHA ☐ Conventional ☐ Other (explain): | | Agency Case Number | Lender Case Number |
| Amount $ | Interest Rate %| No. of Months | **Amortization Type:** ☐ Fixed Rate ☐ GPM | ☐ Other (explain): ☐ ARM (type): |

| II. PROPERTY INFORMATION AND PURPOSE OF LOAN | | | | |
|---|---|---|---|---|
| Subject Property Address (street, city, state & ZIP) | | | | No. of Units |
| Legal Description of Subject Property (attach description if necessary) | | | | Year Built |
| Purpose of Loan  ☐ Purchase ☐ Refinance ☐ Construction  ☐ Construction-Permanent ☐ Other (explain): | | | Property will be: ☐ Primary Residence ☐ Secondary Residence ☐ Investment | |

*Complete this line if construction or construction-permanent loan.*

| Year Lot Acquired | Original Cost | Amount Existing Liens | (a) Present Value of Lot | (b) Cost of Improvements | Total (a + b) |
|---|---|---|---|---|---|
| | $ | $ | $ | $ | $ |

*Complete this line if this is a refinance loan.*

| Year Acquired | Original Cost | Amount Existing Liens | Purpose of Refinance | Describe Improvements | ☐ made ☐ to be made |
|---|---|---|---|---|---|
| | | | | | |

| Title will be held in what Name(s) | Manner in which Title will be held | Estate will be held in: ☐ Fee Simple ☐ Leasehold (show expiration date) |
|---|---|---|
| | | |

| Source of Down Payment, Settlement Charges, and/or Subordinate Financing (explain) |
|---|
| |

☐

| Borrower | III. BORROWER INFORMATION | Co-Borrower |
|---|---|---|

**Borrower's Name** (include Jr. or Sr. if applicable) | **Co-Borrower's Name** (include Jr. or Sr. if applicable)

| Social Security Number | Home Phone (incl. Area code) | DOB (mm/dd/yyyy) | Yrs. School | Social Security Number | Home Phone (incl. Area code) | DOB (mm/dd/yyyy) | Yrs. School |
|---|---|---|---|---|---|---|---|
| | | | | | | | |

| ☐ Married ☐ Separated | Dependents (not listed by Co-Borrower) | ☑ Married ☑ Separated | Dependents (not listed by Borrower) |
|---|---|---|---|
| ☐ Unmarried (include single, divorced, widowed) | no. / ages | ☐ Unmarried (include single, divorced, widowed) | no. / ages |

Present Address (street, city, state, ZIP)   ☐ Own ☐ Rent __No. Yrs. | Present Address (street, city, state, ZIP)   ☐ Own ☐ Rent __No. Yrs.

Mailing Address, if different from Present Address | Mailing Address, if different from Present Address

*If residing at present address for less than two years, complete the following:*

Former Address (street, city, state, ZIP)   ☐ Own ☐ Rent __No. Yrs. | Former Address (street, city, state, ZIP)   ☐ Own ☐ Rent __No. Yrs.

| Borrower | IV. EMPLOYMENT INFORMATION | Co-Borrower |
|---|---|---|

| Name & Address of Employer | ☐ Self Employed | Yrs. on this job | Name & Address of Employer | ☐ Self Employed | Yrs. on this job |
|---|---|---|---|---|---|
| | | Yrs. employed in this line of work/profession | | | Yrs. employed in this line of work/profession |
| Position/Title/Type of Business | | Business Phone (incl. area code) | Position/Title/Type of Business | | Business Phone (incl. area code) |

*If employed in current position for less than two years or if currently employed in more than one position, complete the following:*

| Name & Address of Employer | ☐ Self Employed | Dates (from – to) | Name & Address of Employer | ☐ Self Employed | Dates (from – to) |
|---|---|---|---|---|---|
| | | Monthly Income $ | | | Monthly Income $ |
| Position/Title/Type of Business | | Business Phone (incl. area code) | Position/Title/Type of Business | | Business Phone (incl. area code) |
| Name & Address of Employer | ☐ Self Employed | Dates (from – to) | Name & Address of Employer | ☐ Self Employed | Dates (from – to) |
| | | Monthly Income $ | | | Monthly Income $ |
| Position/Title/Type of Business | | Business Phone (incl. area code) | Position/Title/Type of Business | | Business Phone (incl. area code) |

## V. MONTHLY INCOME AND COMBINED HOUSING EXPENSE INFORMATION

| Gross Monthly Income | Borrower | Co-Borrower | Total | Combined Monthly Housing Expense | Present | Proposed |
|---|---|---|---|---|---|---|
| Base Empl. Income* | $ | $ | $ | Rent | $ | |
| Overtime | | | | First Mortgage (P&I) | | $ |
| Bonuses | | | | Other Financing (P&I) | | |
| Commissions | | | | Hazard Insurance | | |
| Dividends/ Interest | | | | Real Estate Taxes | | |
| Net Rental Income | | | | Mortgage Insurance | | |
| Other (before completing, see the notice in "describe other income," below) | | | | Homeowner Assn. Dues | | |
| | | | | Other: | | |
| Total | $ | $ | $ | Total | $ | $ |

*   Self Employed Borrower(s) may be required to provide additional documentation such as tax returns and financial statements.

| Describe Other Income | Notice: Alimony, child support, or separate maintenance income need not be revealed if the Borrower (B) or Co-Borrower (C) does not choose to have it considered for repaying this loan. | |
|---|---|---|
| B/C | | Monthly Amount |
| | | $ |
| | | |
| | | |
| | | |

## VI. ASSETS AND LIABILITIES

This Statement and any applicable supporting schedules may be completed jointly by both married and unmarried Co-Borrowers if their assets and liabilities are sufficiently joined so that the Statement can be meaningfully and fairly presented on a combined basis; otherwise, separate Statements and Schedules are required. If the Co-Borrower section was completed about a non-applicant spouse or other person, this Statement and supporting schedules must be completed about that spouse or other person also.

Completed ☐ Jointly ☐ Not Jointly

| ASSETS<br><br>Description | Cash or Market Value | Liabilities and Pledged Assets. List the creditor's name, address, and account number for all outstanding debts, including automobile loans, revolving charge accounts, real estate loans, alimony, child support, stock pledges, etc. Use continuation sheet, if necessary. Indicate by (*) those liabilities, which will be satisfied upon sale of real estate owned or upon refinancing of the subject property. | | |
|---|---|---|---|---|
| Cash deposit toward purchase held by: | $ | LIABILITIES | Monthly Payment & Months Left to Pay | Unpaid Balance |
| List checking and savings accounts below | | Name and address of Company | $ Payment/Months | $ |
| Name and address of Bank, S&L, or Credit Union | | | | |
| | | Acct. no. | | |
| Acct. no. | $ | Name and address of Company | $ Payment/Months | $ |
| | | | | |

## VI. ASSETS AND LIABILITIES (cont'd)

| | | | | |
|---|---|---|---|---|
| Name and address of Bank, S&L, or Credit Union | | Acct. no. | | |
| Acct. no. | $ | Name and address of Company | $ Payment/Months | $ |
| Name and address of Bank, S&L, or Credit Union | | | | |
| | | Acct. no. | | |
| Acct. no. | $ | Name and address of Company | $ Payment/Months | $ |
| Name and address of Bank, S&L, or Credit Union | | | | |
| | | Acct. no. | | |
| Acct. no. | $ | Name and address of Company | $ Payment/Months | $ |
| Stocks & Bonds (Company name/number & description) | $ | | | |
| | | Acct. no. | | |
| Life insurance net cash value<br><br>Face amount $ | $ | Name and address of Company | $ Payment/Months | $ |
| **Subtotal Liquid Assets** | $ | Acct. no. | | |
| Real estate owned (enter market value from schedule of real estate owned) | $ | Alimony/Child Support/Separate Maintenance Payments Owned to: | $ | $ |
| Vested interest in retirement fund | $ | | | |
| Net worth of business(es) owned (attach financial statement) | $ | Job-Related Expense (child care, union dues, etc.) | $ | |
| Automobiles owned (make and year) | $ | | | |
| Other Assets (itemize) | $ | | | |
| | | | | |
| | | **Total Monthly Payments** | **$** | |
| **Total Assets**<br>a. | $ | **Net Worth**<br>(a minus b) | $ | **Total Liabilities**<br>b. | $ |
| | | | | |

77

**Schedule of Real Estate Owned** (If additional properties are owned, use continuation sheet.)

| Property Address (enter S if sold, PS if pending sale or R if rental being held for income) | | Type of Property | Present Market Value | Amount of Mortgages & Liens | Gross Rental Income | Mortgage Payments | Insurance, Maintenance, Taxes & Misc. | Net Rental Income |
|---|---|---|---|---|---|---|---|---|
| | | | $ | $ | $ | $ | $ | $ |
| | | | | | | | | |
| | | | | | | | | |
| | Totals | | $ | $ | $ | $ | $ | $ |

List any additional names under which credit has previously been received and indicate appropriate creditor name(s) and account number(s):

| Alternate Name | Creditor Name | Account Number |
|---|---|---|
| | | |

| | VII. DETAILS OF TRANSACTION | | VIII. DECLARATIONS | | Borrower | | Co-Borrower | |
|---|---|---|---|---|---|---|---|---|
| a. | Purchase price | $ | If you answer "Yes" to any questions a through i, please use continuation sheet for explanation. | | | | | |
| b. | Alterations, improvements, repairs | | | | Yes | No | Yes | No |
| c. | Land (if acquired separately) | | a. Are there any outstanding judgments against you? | | ☐ | ☐ | ☐ | ☐ |
| d. | Refinance (incl. debts to be paid off) | | b. Have you been declared bankrupt within the past 7 years? | | ☐ | ☐ | ☐ | ☐ |
| e. | Estimated prepaid items | | c. Have you had property foreclosed upon or given title or deed in lieu thereof in the last 7 years? | | ☐ | ☐ | ☐ | ☐ |
| f. | Estimated closing costs | | d. Are you a party to a lawsuit? | | ☐ | ☐ | ☐ | ☐ |
| g. | PMI, MIP, Funding Fee | | e. Have you directly or indirectly been obligated on any loan of which resulted in foreclosure, transfer of title in lieu of foreclosure, or judgment? (This would include such loans as home mortgage loans, SBA loans, home improvement loans, educational loans, manufactured (mobile) home loans, any mortgage, financial obligation, bond, or loan guarantee. If "Yes," provide details, including date, name, and address of Lender, FHA or VA case number, if any, and reasons for the action.) | | ☐ | ☐ | ☐ | ☐ |
| h. | Discount (if Borrower will pay) | | f. Are you presently delinquent or in default on any Federal debt or any other loan, mortgage, financial obligation, bond, or loan guarantee? If "Yes," give details as described in the preceding question. | | ☐ | ☐ | ☐ | ☐ |
| i. | Total costs (add items a through h) | | g. Are you obligated to pay alimony, child support, or separate maintenance? | | ☐ | ☐ | ☐ | ☐ |

| VII. DETAILS OF TRANSACTION (cont'd) | | | VIII. DECLARATIONS (cont'd) | | | | |
|---|---|---|---|---|---|---|---|
| k. | Borrower's closing costs paid by Seller | | i. Are you a co-maker or endorser on a note? | ☐ | ☐ | ☐ | ☐ |
| l. | Other Credits (explain) | | | | | | |
| | | | j. Are you a U.S. citizen? | ☐ | ☐ | ☐ | ☐ |
| | | | k. Are you a permanent resident alien? | ☐ | ☐ | ☐ | ☐ |
| m. | Loan amount (exclude PMI, MIP, Funding Fee financed) | | l. **Do you intend to occupy the property as your primary residence?** If "Yes," complete question m below. | ☐ | ☐ | ☐ | ☐ |
| n. | PMI, MIP, Funding Fee financed | | m. Have you had an ownership interest in a property in the last three years? | ☐ | ☐ | ☐ | ☐ |
| o. | Loan amount (add m & n) | | (1) What type of property did you own—principal residence (PR), second home (SH), or investment property (IP)? | ___ | ___ | ___ | ___ |
| p. | Cash from/to Borrower (subtract j, k, l & o from i) | | (2) How did you hold title to the home— by yourself (S), jointly with your spouse or jointly with another person (O)? | ___ | ___ | ___ | ___ |

### ACKNOWLEDGMENT AND AGREEMENT

Each of the undersigned specifically represents to Lender and to Lender's actual or potential agents, brokers, processors, attorneys, insurers, servicers, successors and assigns and agrees and acknowledges that: (1) the information provided in this application is true and correct as of the date set forth opposite my signature and that any intentional or negligent misrepresentation of this information contained in this application may result in civil liability, including monetary damages, to any person who may suffer any loss due to reliance upon any misrepresentation that I have made on this application, and/or in criminal penalties including, but not limited to, fine or imprisonment or both under the provisions of Title 18, United States Code, Sec. 1001, et seq.; (2) the loan requested pursuant to this application (the "Loan") will be secured by a mortgage or deed of trust on the property described in this application; (3) the property will not be used for any illegal or prohibited purpose or use; (4) all statements made in this application are made for the purpose of obtaining a residential mortgage loan; (5) the property will be occupied as indicated in this application; (6) the Lender, its servicers, successors or assigns may retain the original and/or an electronic record of this application, whether or not the Loan is approved; (7) the Lender and its agents, brokers, insurers, servicers, successors, and assigns may continuously rely on the information contained in the application, and I am obligated to amend and/or supplement the information provided in this application if any of the material facts that I have represented should change prior to closing of the Loan; (8) in the event that my payments on the Loan become delinquent, the Lender, its servicers, successors or assigns may, in addition to any other rights and remedies that it may have relating to such delinquency, report my name and account information to one or more consumer reporting agencies; (9) ownership of the Loan and/or administration of the Loan account may be transferred with such notice as may be required by law; (10) neither Lender nor its agents, brokers, insurers, servicers, successors or assigns has made any representation or warranty, express or implied, to me regarding the property or the condition or value of the property; and (11) my transmission of this application as an "electronic record" containing my "electronic signature," as those terms are defined in applicable federal and/or state laws (excluding audio and video recordings), or my facsimile transmission of this application containing a facsimile of my signature, shall be as effective, enforceable and valid as if a paper version of this application were delivered containing my original written signature.

Acknowledgement. Each of the undersigned hereby acknowledges that any owner of the Loan, its servicers, successors and assigns, may verify or reverify any information contained in this application or obtain any information or data relating to the Loan, for any legitimate business purpose through any source, including a source named in this application or a consumer reporting agency.

| Borrower's Signature | Date | Co-Borrower's Signature | Date |
|---|---|---|---|
| X | | X | |

laws. You are not required to furnish this information, but are encouraged to do so. The law provides that a lender may not discriminate either on the basis of this information, or on whether you choose to furnish it. If you furnish the information, please provide both ethnicity and race. For race, you may check more than one designation. If you do not furnish ethnicity, race, or sex, under Federal regulations, this lender is required to note the information on the basis of visual observation and surname if you have made this application in person. If you do not wish to furnish the information, please check the box below. (Lender must review the above material to assure that the disclosures satisfy all requirements to which the lender is subject under applicable state law for the particular type of loan applied for.)

| BORROWER | CO-BORROWER |
|---|---|
| ☐ I do not wish to furnish this information | ☐ I do not wish to furnish this information |
| **Ethnicity:** ☐ Hispanic or Latino<br>     ☐ Not Hispanic or Latino | **Ethnicity:** ☐ Hispanic or Latino<br>     ☐ Not Hispanic or Latino |
| **Race:** ☐ American Indian or Alaska Native<br>    ☐ Asian<br>    ☐ Black or African American<br>    ☐ Native Hawaiian or Other Pacific Islander<br>    ☐ White | **Race:** ☐ American Indian or Alaska Native<br>    ☐ Asian<br>    ☐ Black or African American<br>    ☐ Native Hawaiian or Other Pacific Islander<br>    ☐ White |
| **Sex:** ☐ Female   ☐ Male | **Sex:** ☐ Female   ☐ Male |

**To be Completed by Loan Originator**

This information was provided:
- ☐ In a face-to-face interview
- ☐ In a telephone interview
- ☐ By the applicant and submitted by fax or mail
- ☐ By the applicant and submitted via e-mail or the Internet

| Loan Originator's Signature | | Date |
|---|---|---|
| Loan Originator's Name (print or type) | Loan Originator Identifier | Loan Originator's Phone Number (including area code) |
| Loan Origination Company's Name | Loan Origination Company Identifier | Loan Origination Company's Address |

## CONTINUATION SHEET/RESIDENTIAL LOAN APPLICATION

| Use this continuation sheet if you need more space to complete the Residential Loan Application. Mark **B** for Borrower or **C** for Co-Borrower. | Borrower: | Agency Case Number: |
|---|---|---|
| | | |
| | Co-Borrower: | Lender Case Number: |
| | | |

I/We fully understand that it is a Federal crime punishable by fine or imprisonment, or both, to knowingly make any false statements concerning any of the above facts as applicable under the provisions of Title 18, United States Code, Section 1001, et seq.

| Borrower's Signature<br>X | Date | Co-Borrower's Signature<br>X | Date |
|---|---|---|---|

| Uniform Residential Loan Application<br>Freddie Mac Form 65   7/05 (rev.6/09) | Page 8 of 8 | Fannie Mae Form 1003   7/05 (rev.6/09) |

81

# Uniform Underwriting and Transmittal Summary

## I. Borrower and Property Information

Borrower Name _____ SSN _____

Co-Borrower Name _____ SSN _____

Property Address _____

| Property Type | Project Classification | | Occupancy Status | Additional Property Information |
|---|---|---|---|---|
| ☐ 1 unit | **Freddie Mac** **Fannie Mae** | | ☑ Primary Residence | Number of Units _____ |
| ☐ 2-4 units | ☐ III Condo | ☐ P Limited Review New ☐ E PUD ☐ 1 Co-op | ☐ Second Home | Sales Price $ _____ |
| ☐ Condominium | ☐ II Condo | ☐ Q Limited Review Est. ☐ F PUD ☐ 2 Co-op | ☐ Investment Property | Appraised Value $ _____ |
| ☐ PUD ☐ Co-op | ☐ I Condo | ☐ R Expedited New | | |
| ☐ Manufactured Housing | | ☐ S Expedited Est. | | **Property Rights** |
| ☐ Single Wide | | ☐ T Fannie Mae Review | | ☑ Fee Simple |
| ☐ Multiwide | | ☐ U FHA-approved | | ☐ Leasehold |

Project Name _____

## II. Mortgage Information

| Loan Type | Amortization Type | Loan Purpose | Lien Position |
|---|---|---|---|
| ☑ Conventional | ☑ Fixed-Rate—Monthly Payments | ☑ Purchase | ☑ First Mortgage |
| ☐ FHA | ☐ Fixed-Rate—Biweekly Payments | ☐ Cash-Out Refinance | Amount of Subordinate Financing |
| ☐ VA | ☐ Balloon | ☐ Limited Cash-Out Refinance (Fannie) | $ _____ |
| ☐ USDA/RHS | ☐ ARM (type) _____ | ☐ No Cash-Out Refinance (Freddie) | (If HELOC, include balance and credit limit) |
| | ☐ Other (specify) _____ | ☐ Home Improvement | ☐ Second Mortgage |
| | | ☐ Construction to Permanent | |

| Note Information | Mortgage Originator | Buydown | If Second Mortgage |
|---|---|---|---|
| Original Loan Amount $ _____ | ☐ Seller | ☐ Yes | Owner of First Mortgage |
| Initial P&I Payment $ _____ | ☐ Broker | ☑ No | ☐ Fannie Mae ☐ Freddie Mac |
| Initial Note Rate _____ % | ☐ Correspondent | Terms _____ | ☐ Seller/Other |
| Loan Term (in months) _____ | Broker/Correspondent Name and Company Name: | | Original Loan Amount of First Mortgage |
| | _____ | | $ _____ |

## III. Underwriting Information

Underwriter's Name _____     Appraiser's Name/License # _____     Appraisal Company Name _____

**Stable Monthly Income**

Present Housing Payment: $ _____

| | Borrower | Co-Borrower | Total |
|---|---|---|---|
| Base Income | $ _____ | $ _____ | $ _____ |
| Other Income | $ _____ | $ _____ | $ _____ |
| Positive Cash Flow (subject property) | $ _____ | $ _____ | $ _____ |
| Total Income | $ _____ | $ _____ | $ _____ |

**Proposed Monthly Payments**

| Borrower's Primary Residence | |
|---|---|
| First Mortgage P&I | $ _____ |
| Second Mortgage P&I | $ _____ |
| Hazard Insurance | $ _____ |
| Taxes | $ _____ |
| Mortgage Insurance | $ _____ |
| HOA Fees | $ _____ |
| Lease/Ground Rent | $ _____ |
| Other | $ _____ |
| Total Primary Housing Expense | $ _____ |

**Qualifying Ratios**

| | | **Loan-to-Value Ratios** | |
|---|---|---|---|
| Primary Housing Expense/Income | _____ % | LTV | _____ % |
| Total Obligations/Income | _____ % | CLTV/TLTV | _____ % |
| Debt-to-Housing Gap Ratio (Freddie) | _____ % | HCLTV/HTLTV | _____ % |

Other Obligations

Negative Cash Flow (subject property) $ _____

**Qualifying Rate**

**Level of Property Review**

| | | | |
|---|---|---|---|
| ☐ Note Rate | _____ % | ☐ Exterior/Interior | |
| ☐ _____ % Above Note Rate | _____ % | ☐ Exterior Only | |
| ☐ _____ % Below Note Rate | _____ % | ☐ No Appraisal | |
| ☐ Bought-Down Rate | _____ % | Form Number: _____ | |
| ☐ Other | _____ % | | |

All Other Monthly Payments $ _____

Total All Monthly Payments $ _____

**Borrower Funds to Close**

Required $ _____

**Risk Assessment**     **Escrow (T&I)**     Verified Assets $ _____

☐ Manual Underwriting     ☑ Yes ☐ No

☐ AUS

☐ DU ☐ LP ☐ Other _____     Source of Funds _____

AUS Recommendation _____     No. of Months Reserves _____

DU Case ID/LP AUS Key# _____     Interested Party Contributions _____ %

LP Doc Class (Freddie) _____     Community Lending/Affordable Housing Initiative ☐ Yes ☑ No

Representative Credit/Indicator Score _____     Home Buyers/Homeownership Education Certificate in file ☐ Yes ☑ No

**Underwriter Comments** _____

### :::Experian
A world of insight

## Online Personal Credit Report from Experian for

| Experian credit report prepared for | Index: |
|---|---|
| .Mr. Borrower | - Potentially negative items |
| Your report number is | - Accounts in good standing |
| **064065** [1] | - Requests for your credit history |
| Report date: | - Personal information |
| 10/13/2013 | - Important message from Experian [2] |
| | - Contact us |

Experian collects and organizes information about you and your credit history from public records, your creditors and other reliable sources. Experian makes your credit history available to your current and prospective creditors, employers and others as allowed by law, which can expedite your ability to obtain credit and can make offers of credit available to you. We do not grant or deny credit; each credit grantor makes that decision based on its own guidelines.

To return to your report in the near future, log on to www..experian.com/consumer and select "View your report again" or "Dispute" and then enter your report number.

If you disagree with information in this report, return to the Report Summary page and follow the instructions for disputing.

## Potentially Negative Items [3]
back to top

### Public Records

Credit grantors may carefully review the items listed below when they check your credit history. Please note that the account information connected with some public records, such as bankruptcy, also may appear with your credit items listed later in this report.

**MAIN COUNTY CLERK**

| Address: | Identification Number: | Plaintiff: |
|---|---|---|
| 123 Moving Ave | 1 | |
| Chicago, IL. 60000 | | |

| Status: | Status Details: |
|---|---|
| Civil claim paid. | This item was verified and updated in Apr 2007. |

| Date Filed: | Claim Amount: |
|---|---|
| 3/19/2009 | 1,900 |
| Date Resolved: | Liability |
| 6/19/2009 | Amount: NA |
| Responsibility: | |
| INDIVIDUAL | |

**Report number:**

You will need your report number to contact Experian online, by phone or by mail.

**Index:**

Navigate through the sections of your credit report using these links.

**Potentially negative items:**

Items that creditors may view less favorably. It includes the creditor's name and address, your account number (shortened for security), account status, type and terms of the account and any other information reported to Experian by the creditor. Also includes any bankruptcy, lien and judgment information obtained directly from the courts.

**Status:**

Indicates the current status of the account.

## Credit Items

For your protection, the last few digits of your account numbers do not display.

Mr. BorrowerBanking

| Address: | Account Number: |
|---|---|
| 1900 Borower lane | 1000000.... |
| Chicago, IL. 60000 | |

Status: Paid/Past due 60 days.  **4**

| Date Opened: | Type: | Credit Limit/Original Amount: |
|---|---|---|
| 10/2005 | Installment | $523 |
| Reported Since: | Terms: | High Balance: |
| 11/2005 | 12 Months | NA |
| Date of Status: | Monthly | Recent Balance: |
| 04/2007 | Payment: | $0 as of 04/2007 |
| | $0 | Recent Payment: |
| Last Reported: | Responsibility: | $0 |
| 04/2007 | Individual | |

Account History:
60 days as of 12-2006
30 days as of 11-2006

If you believe information in your report is inaccurate, you can dispute that item quickly, effectively and cost free by using Experian's online dispute service located at:

www.experian.com/disputes

Disputing online is the fastest way to address any concern you may have about the information in your credit report.

---

Sample Credit Report


Sample Credit Report                    Page 2 of 4

Borrower's Credit union                    3/19/2009

| Address: | Account Number: | Original Creditor: |
|---|---|---|
| 123 Easy debt | | |
| Chicago, IL. 60000 | 111222IOU | Borrower's Credit union |

Status: Collection account. $95 past due as of 4-2000.

84

**MAIN COLL AGENCIES**

| Address: | Account Number: | Original Creditor: |
|---|---|---|
| Credit union<br>123 Easy debt<br>Chicago, IL. 60000 | 222IOU22 | PayMe Credit union |

Status: Collection account. $95 past due as of 4-2000.

| Date Opened:<br>01/2005 | Type:<br>Installment | Credit Limit/Original Amount:<br>$95 |
|---|---|---|
| Reported Since:<br>04/2005 | Terms:<br>NA | High Balance:<br>NA |
| Date of Status:<br>04/2005 | Monthly<br>Payment:<br>$0 | Recent Balance:<br>$95 as of 04/2005<br>Recent Payment:<br>$0 |
| Last Reported:<br>04/2005 | Responsibility:<br>Individual | |

Your statement: ITEM DISPUTED BY CONSUMER

Account History:
Collection as of 4-2005

04/15/2006

## Accounts in Good Standing     5                          back to top

**AUTOMOBILE AUTO FINANCE**

| Address: | Account Number: | |
|---|---|---|
| 123 Big debt<br>Chicago, IL. 60000 | 12345678998.... | Mr. BorrowerBanking |

Status: Open/Never late.

| Date Opened:<br>04/15/2009 | Type:<br>Installment     6 | Credit Limit/Original Amount:<br>$10,355 |
|---|---|---|
| Reported Since: | Terms:<br>65 Months | High Balance:<br>NA |
| Date of Status: | Monthly<br>Payment:<br>$210 | Recent Balance:<br>$7,984 as of 04/2007<br>Recent Payment:<br>$0 |
| Last Reported: | Responsibility:<br>Individual | |

*Accounts in good standing:*

Lists accounts that have a positive status and may be viewed favorably by creditors. Some creditors do not report to us, so some of your accounts may not be listed.

*Type:*

Account type indicates whether your account is a revolving or an installment account.

85

## Requests for Your Credit History    `7`    back to top

### Requests Viewed By Others

We make your credit history available to your current and prospective creditors and employers as allowed by law. Personal data about you may be made available to companies whose products and services may interest you.

The section below lists all who have requested in the recent past to review your credit history as a result of actions involving you, such as the completion of a credit application or the transfer of an account to a collection agency, application for insurance, mortgage or loan application, etc. Creditors may view these requests when evaluating your creditworthiness.

Address: _____  Date of Request: _____

Comments: _____
_____

Address: _____  Date of Request:
                                            02/23/2006

Comments: _____
_____

Address: _____  Date of Request: _____

Comments: _____
_____

### Requests Viewed Only By You

The section below lists all who have a permissible purpose by law and have requested in the recent past to review your information. You may not have initiated these requests, so you may not recognize each source. We offer information about you to those with a permissible purpose, for example, to:

- other creditors who want to offer you preapproved credit;
- an employer who wishes to extend an offer of employment;
- a potential investor in assessing the risk of a current obligation;
- Experian or other credit reporting agencies to process a report for you;
- your existing creditors to monitor your credit activity (date listed may reflect only the most recent request).

We report these requests **only to you** as a record of activities. We **do not** provide this information to other creditors who evaluate your creditworthiness.

Address: _____  Date of Request: _____

Address: _____  Date of Request: _____

Address: _____  Date of Request: _____

---

*Requests for your credit history:*

Also called "inquiries," requests for your credit history are logged on your report whenever anyone reviews your credit information. There are two types of inquiries.

i.
Inquiries resulting from a transaction initiated by you. These include inquiries from your applications for credit, insurance, housing or other loans. They also include transfer of an account to a collection agency. Creditors may view these items when evaluating your creditworthiness.

ii.
Inquiries resulting from transactions you may not have initiated but that are allowed under the FCRA. These include preapproved offers, as well as for employment, investment review, account monitoring by existing creditors, and requests by you for your own report. These items are shown only to you and have no impact on your creditworthiness or risk scores.

86

**Disclosure of Information on Lead-Based Paint or Hazards**

## Lead Warning Statement

Housing built before 1978 may contain lead-based paint. Lead from paint, paint chips and dust can pose health hazards if not managed properly. Lead exposure is especially harmful to young children and pregnant women. Before renting pre-1978 housing, lessors must disclose the presence of known lead-based paint and/or lead-based hazards in the dwelling. Lessees must also receive a federally approved pamphlet on lead poisoning prevention.

**Lessor's Disclosure**

**(a) Presence of lead-based paint and/or lead-based paint hazards. Check (i) or (ii) below:**

____ (i) Known lead-based paint and/or lead-based paint hazards are present in the housing (explain): _____ .

____ (ii) Lessor has no knowledge of lead-based paint and/or lead-based paint hazards in the housing.

**(b) Records and reports available to the lessor. Check (i) or (ii) below:**

____ (i) Lessor has provided the lessee with all available records and reports pertaining to lead-based paint and/or lead-based paint hazards in the housing (list documents below):

_____ .

(ii) Lessor has no reports or records pertaining to lead-based paint or lead-based paint hazards in the housing.

**Lessee's Acknowledgment (initial)**

(c)_____ Lessee has received copies of all information listed above.

(d)_____ Lessee has received the pamphlet Protect Your Family from Lead in Your Home.

**Agent's Acknowledgment (initial)**

(e)_____ Agent has informed the lessor of the lessor's obligations under 42 USC 4852d and is aware of his/her responsibility to ensure compliance.

**Certification of Accuracy**

The following parties have reviewed the information above and certify, to the best of their knowledge, that the information they have provided is true and accurate.

| _____ | _____ | _____ |
|---|---|---|
| Lessor | Date | Lessor |
| | Date | |
| | | |
| _____ | _____ | _____ |
| Lessee | Date | Lessee |
| | Date | |
| _____ | _____ | _____ |
| **Agent** | **Date** | **Agent** | **Date** |

Instructions for Obtaining Title Insurance

Title Insurance Company
 American Ordering Procedures (American)
 American Names and Phone Numbers (First American Phone)
Scott Title Guaranty Company
Scott Ordering Procedures (Scott)
Scott Names and Phone Numbers (Scott Phone)

**Title Insurance Company**
**TITLE, ESCROW AND RELATED SERVICES**
**ORDER PLACEMENT AND PROCEDURES**
**Pre-Closing**
Borrower applies for loan with Lender ("Lender").
Lender places order with First American's High Volume Commercial Unit
(hereinafter "HVCU") located at: 3101 Main Drive, Suite 42
Kissimmee, FL  34647 (407) 452-3691   Fax (407) 452-3692
HVCU will process orders for all products requested (i.e. title and escrow, survey
(if necessary), appraisal or flood certification) through the Dallas HVCU office.
HVCU hours of operation are 8:30 a.m. – 7:00 p.m., CST, to accommodate customers
**NOTE**:  A list of office staff with job descriptions is attached for your convenience.

HVCU places the appropriate orders and monitors their progress.

HVCU provides an order confirmation to Lender, which includes estimated prices for the
products ordered.

HVCU receives products from field offices in required time frame.
Non-title products are forwarded to Lender.
Upon receipt of title insurance commitment, HVCU
reviews commitment for completeness of underlying documents;
reviews commitment for conformity to lender requirements;
underwrites for necessary endorsements and affirmative coverage;  and
prepares revisions to the commitment, as necessary.

HVCU will work with the Lender to:
delete the survey exception and provide an ALTA 9 **without a survey**;
obtain zoning letters from local jurisdiction for issuance of the ALTA 3.1;  and
resolve title issues.

# I. Closing

    A. HVCU obtains pay-off information from existing lender.

    B. HVCU prepares settlement statement.

    C. Settlement takes place through the mail; or

    D. Settlement takes place as an accommodation sign-up.

    NOTE: "Accommodation Sign-Ups" are conducted by ONE First American designated office per metropolitan area based on:

        1. Economies of Scale

        2. Familiarity with Program

    E. A marked-up commitment is provided at closing.

    F. HVCU causes documents to be recorded.

    G. HVCU disburses funds.

# II. Post Closing

    A. Policies are typed from mark-ups.

    B. Releases for paid off loans are obtained and recorded.

**National Accounts**
**High Volume Commercial Unit**
Operations: 3101 Main Drive, Suite 42
Kissimmee, FL  34647
(407) 452-3691
Fax (407) 452-3692

| Jess Hahl0n | Vice President & Manager | x6900 |
|---|---|---|
| Cathy Stewart | Counsel/Escrow Officer | x7022 |
| Richard Murphys | Escrow Officer/Production Manager | x7019 |
| Bernice Powns | Escrow Officer | x7018 |
| William Lindson | Post Closer | N/A |
| Mac  Celeivy | Accountant | x6826 |
| John  Marrison | Accountant/Administrative Assistant | N/A |
| Diane. Sanders | Order Entry | x7039 |
| Freddie Mac | Clerical | x7021 |

# III.

**Marketing:**
3101 Main Drive, Suite 42
Kissimmee, FL  34647
(407) 452-3691
Fax (407) 452-3692

| | | |
|---|---|---|
| Hannah Manion | Vice President & Director of Marketing | N/A |
| Rachel Wales | Executive Assistant | N/A |

Stewart Title
Title, Escrow and Related Services
Order Placement and Procedures

Lender to provide necessary information (e.g., prior title policy, legal description, address, existing mortgage information, and entity names) to begin closing process (title abstract, UCC, tax lien and judgment searches) to Scott Title – National Title Office in Kissimmee, Florida ("Scott National Office"), via telephone, fax, e-mail or website, as follows:

**Scott Title Guaranty Company**
3101 Main Drive, Suite 42
Kissimmee, FL  34647
(407) 452-3691
Fax (407) 452-3692
E-mail: mailto:hannah@Scott.com
Website:  www.Scott-nts.com (click on "Commercial" tab and then "Title Order Form")

Scott National Office will notify Lender of the Title Order Number and the name of the assigned Closing Processor.

Scott National Office works with appropriate Scott Title Guaranty Company local office or agent ("Scott Local Office") to obtain title work and tax, county UCC and judgment lien search results and orders appropriate payoff letters, state UCC searches and flood determination letter.

Scott National Office will request an inspection of Property to be done by Scott Local Office for removal of survey exception items from commitment.

Scott Local Office will notify Scott National Office if unable to remove survey exceptions from title commitment based on Property inspection.

When title work is received, Scott National Office will send to the appropriate parties (e.g., Lender and Borrower) the title commitment/title report and a complete set of all underlying documents and will work with Lender and Borrower to clear any and all inapplicable title exceptions.

Scott National Office will coordinate delivery of title commitment update to reflect any necessary changes to the title commitment.

Scott National Office will forward search results to parties when state UCC searches and flood determination reports are received.

Scott National Office will request draft closing instructions from Lender.

If closing is to be in the <u>Lender's office</u>, Lender will notify Scott National Office with date of proposed closing.

If closing is to be in <u>Scott Local Office</u>, Lender sets tentative closing date and notifies Scott National Office of same.

Scott National Office will notify Scott Local Office to call Borrower and set up a <u>Witness</u> <u>Only</u> closing time.

Scott National Office begins drafting closing statement or invoice.

If closing is to occur at Scott Local Office, then loan documents (other than recordable documents) will be returned to Lender and all recordable documents are held by the Scott Local Office until Lender notifies Scott National Office that all loan conditions are met and funds will be wired to Scott National Office.

When funds from Lender are received by Scott National Office, Scott National Office will wire all recording funds, including any property, mortgage or transfer tax funds, to Scott Local Office and authorize recordation of the loan documents.

Scott Local Office notifies Scott National Office that recording has been accomplished and provides recording information to Scott National Office. Scott National Office (i) notifies Lender of recording and provides recording information, (ii) disburses loan proceeds and (iii) pays off prior mortgages and liens.

Scott National Office notifies Lender and Scott Local Office of disbursement of loan and requests Scott Local Office to prepare final title policy. When final title policy is prepared, it is sent to Scott National Office for review.

Scott National Office reviews and forwards title policy to Lender.

**Resources**

If there are going to be any issues with the loan, it is likely to happen in viewing the HUD1, Note or TIL.

Should you need additional help understanding any of these documents, see our how to section or resource section. If you cannot find the help in those two sections, please browse through Fannie Mae and Freddie Mac websites. They have an incredible learning website database for anyone to use for training or gaining mortgage knowledge.

**Federal Regulations & Compliance:**

**FHA insured loan:** is a US Federal Housing Administration mortgage insurance backed mortgage loan which is provided by a FHA-approved lender. FHA insured loans are a type of federal assistance and have historically allowed lower income Americans to borrow money for the purchase of a home that they would not otherwise be able to afford. To obtain mortgage insurance from the Federal Housing Administration, an upfront *mortgage insurance premium* (UFMIP) equal to 1.75 percent of the base loan amount at closing is required, and is normally financed into the total loan amount by the lender and paid to FHA on the borrower's behalf. There is also a monthly mortgage insurance premium (MIP) which varies based on the amortization term and loan-to-value ratio. The program originated during the Great Depression of the 1930s, when the rates of foreclosures and defaults rose sharply, and the program was intended to provide lenders with sufficient insurance. Some FHA programs were subsidized by the government, but the goal was to make it self-supporting, based on insurance premiums paid by borrowers. Over time, private mortgage insurance (PMI) companies came into play, and now FHA primarily serves people who cannot afford a conventional down payment or otherwise do not qualify for PMI. The program has since this time been modified to accommodate the heightened recession.

**Mortgage insurance** is an insurance policy designed to protect the mortgagee (lender) from any default by the mortgagor (borrower). It is used commonly in loans with a loan-to-value ratio over 80%, and employed in the event of foreclosure and repossession. This policy is typically paid for by the borrower as a component to final nominal (note) rate, or in one lump sum up front, or as a separate and itemized component of monthly mortgage payment. In the last case, mortgage insurance can be dropped when the lender informs the borrower, or its subsequent assigns, that the property has appreciated, the loan has been paid down, or any combination of both to relegate the loan-to-value under 80%. In the event of repossession, banks, investors, etc. must resort to selling the property to recoup their original investment (the money lent), and are able to dispose of hard assets (such as real estate) more quickly by reductions in price. Therefore, the

93

mortgage insurance acts as a hedge should the repossessing authority recover less than full and fair market value for any hard asset.

**Mortgage Loan types-**
There are many types of mortgages used worldwide, but several factors broadly define the characteristics of the mortgage. All of these may be subject to local regulation and legal requirements.

**The two basic types of amortized loans** are the fixed rate mortgage (FRM) and adjustable-rate mortgage (ARM) (also known as a floating rate or variable rate mortgage). In some countries, such as the United States, fixed rate mortgages are the norm, but floating rate mortgages are relatively common. Combinations of fixed and floating rate mortgages are also common, whereby a mortgage loan will have a fixed rate for some period, for example the first five years, and vary after the end of that period.

**In a fixed rate mortgage**, the interest rate, remains fixed for the life (or term) of the loan. In case of an annuity repayment scheme, the periodic payment remains the same amount throughout the loan. In case of linear payback, the periodic payment will gradually decrease.

**In an adjustable rate mortgage**, the interest rate is generally fixed for a period of time, after which it will periodically (for example, annually or monthly) adjust up or down to some market index. Adjustable rates transfer part of the interest rate risk from the lender to the borrower, and thus are widely used where fixed rate funding is difficult to obtain or prohibitively expensive. Since the risk is transferred to the borrower, the initial interest rate may be, for example, 0.5% to 2% lower than the average 30-year fixed rate; the size of the price differential will be related to debt market conditions, including the yield curve. The charge to the borrower depends upon the credit risk in addition to the interest rate risk. The mortgage origination and underwriting process involves checking credit scores, debt-to-income, downpayments, and assets. Jumbo mortgages and subprime lending are not supported by government guarantees and face higher interest rates. Other innovations described below can affect the rates as well.

**Loan to value**
Upon making a mortgage loan for the purchase of a property, lenders usually require that the borrower make a downpayment; that is, contribute a portion of the cost of the property. This downpayment may be expressed as a portion of the value of the property (see below for a definition of this term). The loan to value ratio (or LTV) is the size of the loan against the value of the property. Therefore, a mortgage loan in which the purchaser has made a downpayment of 20% has a loan to value ratio of 80%. For loans made

against properties that the borrower already owns, the loan to value ratio will be imputed against the estimated value of the property.

The loan to value ratio is considered an important indicator of the riskiness of a mortgage loan: the higher the LTV, the higher the risk that the value of the property (in case of foreclosure) will be insufficient to cover the remaining principal of the loan.

**Value: appraised**, estimated, and actual

Since the value of the property is an important factor in understanding the risk of the loan, determining the value is a key factor in mortgage lending. The value may be determined in various ways, but the most common are:

Actual or transaction value: this is usually taken to be the purchase price of the property. If the property is not being purchased at the time of borrowing, this information may not be available.

**Appraised or surveyed value**: in most jurisdictions, some form of appraisal of the value by a licensed professional is common. There is often a requirement for the lender to obtain an official appraisal.

Estimated value: lenders or other parties may use their own internal estimates, particularly in jurisdictions where no official appraisal procedure exists, but also in some other circumstances.

**Payment and debt ratios**

In most countries, a number of more or less standard measures of creditworthiness may be used. Common measures include payment to income (mortgage payments as a percentage of gross or net income); debt to income (all debt payments, including mortgage payments, as a percentage of income); and various net worth measures. In many countries, credit scores are used in lieu of or to supplement these measures. There will also be requirements for documentation of the creditworthiness, such as income tax returns, pay stubs, etc. the specifics will vary from location to location.

Some lenders may also require a potential borrower have one or more months of "reserve assets" available. In other words, the borrower may be required to show the availability of enough assets to pay for the housing costs (including mortgage, taxes, etc.) for a period of time in the event of the job loss or other loss of income.

Many countries have lower requirements for certain borrowers, or "no-doc" / "low-doc" lending standards that may be acceptable in certain circumstances.

Standard or conforming mortgages.

Many countries have a notion of standard or conforming mortgages that define a perceived acceptable level of risk, which may be formal or informal, and may be reinforced by laws, government intervention, or market practice. For example, a standard mortgage may be considered to be one with no more than 70-80% LTV and no more than one-third of gross income going to mortgage debt.

A standard or conforming mortgage is a key concept as it often defines whether or not the mortgage can be easily sold or securitized, or, if non-standard, may affect the price at which it may be sold. In the United States, a conforming mortgage is one which meets the established rules and procedures of the two major government-sponsored entities in the housing finance market (including some legal requirements). In contrast, lenders who decide to make nonconforming loans are exercising a higher risk tolerance and do so knowing that they face more challenge in reselling the loan. Many countries have similar concepts or agencies that define what are "standard" mortgages. Regulated lenders (such as banks) may be subject to limits or higher risk weightings for non-standard mortgages. For example, banks and mortgage brokerages in Canada face restrictions on lending more than 80% of the property value; beyond this level, mortgage insurance is generally required.

**Here are some additional information pieces about a closing:**

**Closing.** The borrowers and the seller finalize all the terms in the contract — and the property is all their! The seller gives the borrowers the title in exchange for the contract purchase price. He also delivers a deed, title evidence and insurance, the property's plat of survey, leases (if applicable) and proof of any required repairs based on the home inspection. It's recommended that you attend the closing with an experienced real estate attorney.

**Escrow closing.** When all the aspects and documents related to the transfer of the property from the seller to borrowers is finalized (similar to a closing). Escrow agents may be title companies, attorneys, trust or escrow companies. Check with the laws in your state to see if escrow closings are legal, and if so, what the procedures are for holding one.

**Survey.** Borrowers should receive a new property survey, or plat, when they buy a home. This diagram legally confirms the exact property boundaries and dimensions of their home.

**Title.** The legal document that says the borrowers own the property. Inquire about the different ways they can hold a title in their state (for example, owning a home with someone else).

**Title insurance.** This is given to the borrowers, and then they have to submit it to the mortgage processor for the lender. The insurance policy is issued after a search for a property's public records, which includes liens, conditions, restrictions and other matters that might affect the marketability of the title.

**Deed.** The document that conveys the title of ownership of a property.

**IRS Form 1099.** The closing agent must report all real estate transactions to the Internal Revenue Service.

**Real Estate Settlement Act.** A form known as the HUD-1 statement, or the Uniform Settlement Statement, is required in all residential real estate transactions with full disclosure of all settlement costs. This form applies to those loans financed by all U.S. government-related mortgage loans.

**Closing statements.** Part of the HUD-1 statement, this lists all itemized payments and credits of a buyer-and-seller transaction. Real estate brokerages or attorneys prepare closing statements.

**Prorations.** Some expenses or items related to the property or mortgage loan are prepaid or paid in arrears must be prorated between the buyer, seller or mortgage lender at closing. Real estate taxes, condominium assessments and utility costs are common expenses that are prorated between the parties.

**Homeowners insurance.** Most mortgage lenders require that the borrowers provide proof (known as a "binder") that they have homeowners insurance on the property they're buying.

**Certified checks.** Most closing agents require certified checks for any payments due at closing. These checks are proof that the money is available when the check is presented.

**Photo identification.** All closing agents require the borrowers bring a photo I.D. to the closing.

**Common closing costs**
**Title:** $500-$900
**Title insurance:** $300-$500
**Recording fees:** $150-$300
**Mortgage:** $700-$2,000
**Attorney:** $400-$2,000
**Real estate transfer taxes:** Varies by location
**Homeowners insurance:** $200-$2,000
**The Loan Closing**

**Settlement Statement - HUD-1 Form:**

A Form required by Federal law and is prepared by the closing agent, and submitted with the borrower's file to underwriting. It provides the details of the sale transaction including the sale price, the amount of financing, loan fees and charges, prorating of real estate taxes, amounts due to and from buyer and seller and funds due to third parties such as the selling real estate agent. It must be signed by both buyer and seller and becomes a part of the lender's permanent loan file.

Some of the borrower's charges on the HUD-1 may have already been paid, such as credit report and appraisal fees. They will be noted as P.O.C. (paid outside the closing). Borrowers will usually be charged interest on the loan from the date of settlement until the first day of the next month. Their first payment will be due on the first day of the month and will be due on the first of the following month. Make sure the borrowers know exactly when their first and future payments are due and what the penalties are for being late.

If the borrower's loan is greater than 80 percent of the value of the property, they will have to pay for mortgage insurance that protects the lender, in case they default. One year's premium will usually run- between 0.5 percent to 0.75 percent of the loan amount.

In addition to their monthly payments on the loan, most lenders will require them to maintain an "escrow", or "impound," account for real estate taxes and insurance. Current law permits a lender to collect 1/6th (2 months) of the estimated annual real estate taxes and insurance payments at closing. Additionally, real estate taxes for the current year will be pro-rated between the borrowers and the seller and paid at closing. After closing, they will remit 1/12 of the annual amount with each monthly payment. Tax and insurance bills should be sent to the lender who will pay them out of the escrow funds collected.

**Truth-in-Lending Statement (TIL):**
Federal law also requires this form. The borrowers were given an initial TIL shortly after they completed the loan application. If no changes have taken place since that time, the lender need not provide one at closing. If, however there are significant charges, they must receive a corrected TIL no later than settlement.

**The Mortgage Note:**
The mortgage note is legal evidence of the borrower's indebtedness and their formal promise to repay the debt. It sets out the amount and terms of the loan and also recites the penalties and steps the lender can take if the borrowers fail to make their payments on time.

**The Mortgage or Deed of Trust:**
This is the "security instrument" which gives the lender a claim against the borrower's house if they fail to live up to the terms of the mortgage note. It recites the legal rights

and obligations of both the borrower and the lender and gives the lender the right to take the property by foreclosure if they should default on the loan. The mortgage or deed of trust will be recorded, providing public notice of the lender's claim (lien) on the property.

## Processing Documents/Loan Underwriting

### Document Preparation

Document Preparation or Doc Prep is the process of arranging and preparing the borrowers closing contracts. These documents vary from industry to industry but generally contain a note, disclosures, and other documents describing and detailing the agreement between the borrower and lender.

**Mortgage Underwriting** - An underwriter is a person who evaluates the loan documentation and determines whether or not the loan complies with the guidelines of the particular mortgage program. It is the underwriter's responsibility to assess the risk of the loan and decide to approve or decline the loan. A processor is the one who gathers and submits the loan documents to the underwriter. Underwriters take at least 48 hours to underwrite the loan and after the borrower signs the package it takes 24 hours for a processor to process the documents.

**Loan origination** - is the process by which a borrower applies for a new loan, and a lender processes that application. Origination generally includes all the steps from taking a loan application up to disbursal of funds (or declining the application). Loan servicing covers everything after disbursing the funds until the loan is fully paid off. Loan origination is a specialized version of new account opening for financial services organizations. Certain people and organizations specialize in loan origination. Mortgage brokers and other mortgage originator companies serve as a prominent example.

### Types of Loans

There are many different types of loans. For more information on loan types, see the loan and consumer lending articles. Steps involved in originating a loan vary by loan type, various kinds of loan risk, regulator, lender policy, and other factors.

**Application Process-** Applications for loans may be made through several different channels and the length of the application process, from initial application to funding, means that different organizations may use various channels for customer interactions over time. In general, loan applications may be split into three distinct types:
Agent assisted (branch-based)
Agent assisted (telephone-based)
Broker sale (third-party sales agent)
Self-service –

**Retail loans and mortgages-** are typically highly competitive products that may not offer a large margin to their providers, but through high volume sales can be highly profitable. The business model of the individual financial institution and the products they offer therefore affects on which application model they will offer

**Agent Assisted** (Branch-Based) Loan Application
The typical types of financial services organizations offering loans through the face to face channel have a long-term investment in 'brick and mortar' branches. Typically these are:
Banks
Credit Unions
Building Societies

**Self-service Loan Application-**
- Self-service web applications are taken in a variety of ways, and the state of this business has evolved over time
- Print and fax applications or pre-qualification forms. Some financial institutions still use these.
Print, write or type data into the form, send it to the financial institution
Form fill on the web, print, and send to the financial institution (not much better)
- Web forms filled out and saved by the applicant on the web site, that are then sent to or retrieved by (ostensibly securely) the financial institution
- True web applications with interfaces to a loan origination system on the back end
- Many of the early solutions had a lot of the same problems as general forms (bad work flows, trying to handle all manner of loan types in one form)
- Wizard-style applications that are very intuitive and don't ask superfluous questions.
Jobs the online application should perform:

1. Present required disclosures, comply with various lending regulations)
2. Be compliant with security requirements (such as Multi-Factor Authentication) where applicable.
3. Collect the necessary applicant data
    1. Exactly what is needed varies by loan type. The application should not ask for data the applicant doesn't absolutely have to provide to get to a pre-qualification decision for the loan type(s) they seek.
    2. The application should pre-fill demographic data if the applicant is an existing client and has logged in.

4. Make it easy, quick, and friendly for the applicant (so they actually complete the application and don't abandon)
5. Get a current credit report
6. Pre-qualify (auto-decision) the application and return a quick response to the applicant. Typically this would be approved subject to stipulations, referred to the financial institution, declined (many FIs shy away from this preferring to refer any application that can't be automatically pre-approved.)

**Loan Specific Compliance Requirements**

Many of the customer identification and due diligence requirements of loan origination are common to new account opening of other financial products.
The following sections describe the specific requirements of loans and mortgages.

**Cross Selling, Add-on Selling**
- Add-on Credit insurance & debt cancellation
- Credit cross selling
- Up-selling
- Down-selling
- Refinancing
- Loan Recapture

**Notes:**

# National Component Prep-test A, B, C

## Answers following test

## National Component Prep-test A, B, C

**Important note about this prep-test:**
Some of this test is above the position of the basic loan processor.
Some questions presented in this prep--test may not be available in this book because they may not apply to the loan processor. However, we recommend you please check for them in the books glossary or google the questions.
The more you know, the further you will go.

**National Component Test A**
TILA allows consumers _____ to back out of a loan transaction through a right of rescission.

- ○ 5 Business days
- ○ 3 Business days
- ○ 7 Business days
- ○ 9 Business days

Fixed-Rate Conventional Mortgages are often referred to as?

- ○ 9 Business days
- ○ 15-yr or 30-yr mortgage loans
- ○ 25-yr or 50-yr mortgage loans
- ○ 5-yr or 20-yr mortgage loans

What is a disadvantage of a Fixed-Rate Mortgage loan?

- ○ Interest rates are slightly lower than ARMs and other special mortgages
- ○ Interest rates are slightly lower than special mortgages
- ○ Interest rates are usually slightly higher than ARMs and other special mortgages
- ○ ARMs are higher than Interest rates

Before a loan is ready to be underwritten, the following MUST be completed:

○ Validated loan application, confirmation on the value of the property, and a title search

○ Validated loan application, monthly income confirmed, purchase of title

○ Evaluation of credit score, salary checked, debt obligations considered

○ Satisfactory down payment, evaluation of past and present loans, assurance of continued income

A title report does NOT include information on ___ .

○ Property description

○ Tax rate

○ Property history

○ Liens

Who ensures the accuracy of a title report?

○ The insurance company

○ The title company

○ An abstractor attorney

○ An escrow company

If a lender charges a document preparation fee, where will it appear?

○ Direct Loan Costs section of the HUD-2

○ Loan Fees Costs section of the HUD-1.

○ Fees Costs section of the HUD-2

○ Loan Fees/Direct Loan Costs section of the HUD-1

Which section of GLB Act prohibits the practice of accessing private information using false pretenses?

○ Safeguards Rule

○ Pretexting Provisions

○ Privacy Provisions

○ Spoofing Provisions

What does BPO stand for?

○ Business Process Outside

○ Beneficiaries Payment Options

○ Brokers Price Option

Who is appointed temporarily under the revenue laws to value where there is no resident appraiser?

○ Any appraiser

○ A valuer

○ Merchant appraiser

○ Resident appraiser

What does HCFP stand for?

○ Health and Community Facilities Programs

○ Housing and Community Facilities Projects

○ Housing and Commonality Facilities Programs

○ Housing and Community Facilities Programs

Under HCFP who does the borrower work with directly?

○ Directly with the HCFP

○ A private lender, such as a bank or credit union

○ A Federally appointed lender

○ Only a Credit Union certified by the HCFP

How many days does MDIA give to creditors to provide good faith estimates of mortgage loan costs?

○ Three Business Days

○ Two Business Days

○ Five Business Days

○ Twenty Business Days

When was the Mortgage Disclosure Improvement Act enacted?

○ The Mortgage Disclosure Improvement Act enacted in July 2007

○ The Mortgage Disclosure Improvement Act enacted in July 2006

○ The Mortgage Disclosure Improvement Act enacted in July 2008

○ The Mortgage Disclosure Improvement Act enacted in July 2005

If a borrower's rent payments are $1,000 per month and the borrower's total monthly income is $4,000. The PHE to Income Ratio is ___?

○ 28%

○ 20%

○ 25%

○ 30%

In what instance would the closing agent open a new escrow account?

○ To cover the closing costs

○ To cover legal fees

○ Under no circumstances

○ If the lender is covering the annual property taxes and insurance payments

What is the main purpose of FHA?

○ To insure residential mortgage loans made by individual/private lenders

○ To set standards for construction

○ To set standards for underwriting

○ To provide loans to borrowers

A Conditional License issued to a salesperson may remain suspended for how many months for failing to submit transcripts?

○ 24

○ 36

○ 18

○ 12

Morality appears to be _____ and _____ in nature

○ Subjective and intuitive

○ Esoteric and qualitative

○ Learned and forgotten

○ Black and white

## National Component Test B

What does FFIEC stand for?

○ Federal Funding and Institutional Equity Capital

○ Future of Foreclosure and Integrated Equal Credit

○ Federal Fixed Insurance and Economy Control

○ Federal Financial Institutions Examination Council

Which year was Truth in Lending Act Enacted?

○ Truth in Lending Act Enacted in 1968

○ Truth in Lending Act Enacted in 1978

○ Truth in Lending Act Enacted in 1958

○ Truth in Lending Act Enacted in 1969

How do you determine your net worth?

○ Subtract the amount of your car loan from the resale value of your car.

○ Subtract your total credit card debt from the balance in your checking account.

○ Subtract your total liabilities from your total assets.

○ Subtract your monthly taxes from your monthly income.

To find the index date, what should you refer to first?

- Week and Time
- A multi-year calendar
- Rate Change Worksheet
- ARM's rate adjustment index

What are the three sections of Gramm-Leach-Bliley Act?

- The three sections of Gramm-Leach-Bliley Act are: Privacy statement, Wealth disclosure statement and Re-funding statement.
- The three sections of Gramm-Leach-Bliley Act are: Financial Modernization Act, Mortgage of assets Act and Regulatory Collection Act.
- The three sections of Gramm-Leach-Bliley Act are: Financial Privacy Rule, Safeguards Rule, and Pretexting provisions.
- The three sections of Gramm-Leach-Bliley Act are: Prohibition of donations, Withdrawal of deposits and Payment of annual bonus.

Mortgage in itself is not a debt, but is a borrower's security for a loan?

- A mortgage in itself is a debt; it is the lender's security for a debt.
- A mortgage in itself is not a debt; it is the lender's security for a debt.
- A mortgage in itself is not a security; it is the borrower's debt for a loan.
- A mortgage in itself is not a loan; it is the lender's debt for a security.

Who is an underwriter?

- The borrower.
- A person who verifies the accuracy of mortgage documents
- The guarantor, who guarantees mortgage.
- A private lender

The Mortgage Disclosure Improvement Act (MDIA) seeks to inform consumers about....

- Estimated mortgage loan costs
- Mortgage loans
- Their credit history

○ Approximate mortgage fees

Does the buyer necessarily need to pay the premium for the lender's title insurance policy?

○ Yes

○ No, he never needs to pay for the lender's title insurance policy.

○ No, not necessarily.

○ It depends on his choice.

Which of the following is the lender's responsibility?

○ Provide a comprehensive list of all the costs you may face.

○ Contact the buyer and arrange meeting times.

○ Email you when there is a suspected change in cost.

○ Preparing estimate of costs you may incur when buying or refinancing

The lender collects and holds taxes in what type of account?

○ Savings

○ Checking

○ Trust

○ Escrow

What reduces the amount of money that can be borrowed by most home buyers?

○ Higher interest rates

○ Lower interest rates

○ Higher Mortgage Value

○ Lower Mortgage Value

What is the purpose of RESPA?

○ To protect lenders from unqualified borrowers

○ To protect borrowers from improper lending practices

○ To make it easier to lend money

○ To keep lenders from having relationships with service providers

What does RESPA stand for?

○ Revolutionary Emerging Socialistic Pattern of Africa

○ Regional Enterprise Security Planning Act.

○ Regular Educational Service Program Act

○ Real Estate Settlement and Procedures Act.

Who benefits from RESPA?

○ Borrowers

○ Lender

○ Both Borrowers and Lenders

○ Neither Borrowers nor Lenders

Failure to submit transcripts will result in _____

○ A fine of $25.00

○ A delay in issuing the license

○ Being denied a license

○ The automatic suspension of the conditional license

Name the two parts which makes the interest rate of ARM (Adjustable rate mortgage).

○ Cost and Income

○ Index and Margin

○ Fixed and Variable

○ Variable and Margin

What is the extra amount, which the lender adds to the index?

○ Cost of Fund Index

○ Margin

○ An Interest-only (I-O) ARM

○ Settlement

How do you calculate the future value of investment in loan calculation?

○ FV (rate, nper [, pmt] [, pv] [, type])

○ PV/ (pmt, rate)

○ FV (rate/PV, pmt, type)

○ PV (pmt/FV*pmt, type)

Which of the following statements about the 1003 Mortgage Application are true?

○ The 1003 Mortgage Application will generally list the borrower employment, unless the application is for a No Employment Verification Loan.

○ A 1003 Mortgage Application is the standard application filled out by a mortgage professional on behalf of a borrower applying for a mortgage loan.

○ Some lenders have the complete 1003 application on their websites.

○ All of the statements are correct.

What is the purpose of a 1003 Mortgage application?

○ It is an application to apply for a mortgage to buy an industrial building.

○ It is an application to modify your mortgage payments.

○ It is a verification application to help the lenders determine whether or not you will be able to pay off your mortgage

○ It is an application that you need to fill out if you are going to let someone assume your mortgage.

MDIA is the abbreviation for?

○ Mortgage Distribution Information Act

○ Mortgage Disclosure Improvement Act

○ Monetary Digitization Information Act

○ Monthly Development Index Act

Which of the following factors does not determine the cost of home insurance?

○ The details about the heirs of the owner.

○ How much value you insure your home for.

○ The age and condition of your property.

○ The location of your home (fire hydrant protection, quality of Fire Department, etc

Which of the following statements is not correct?

○ Hazard insurance is a generic term, referring to property insurance on your home.

○ Flood Insurance is available only through the National Flood Insurance Plan (NFIP).

○ Broader insurance coverage generally costs more than the lender required coverage.

○ All of the above.


## National Component Test C –

What's the abbreviation for?

COE is an abbreviation for?

○ Cost of Eligibility

○ Certificate of Encumbrance

○ Certificate of Education

○ Certificate Of Eligibility

Who is eligible for VA home loan benefits?

○ US military personnel

○ Honorably discharged veterans

○ active military

○ All of the above

Who informs the buyer about the amount of funds to bring to the closing?

○ The insurance company

○ The closing agent

○ The buyer's lender

○ The seller's agent

Which of the following statements is false?

○ The buyer's or borrower's main function at a closing is to review and sign the many documents related to the new mortgage, and to pay closing costs (if applicable to the transaction)

○ Some states have laws that require funding to occur 24-hours after closing

○ In most states, attorneys in law offices conduct the closing.

○ A normal closing takes about one to two hours to complete

Closing costs may be paid by:

○ The seller or the buyer

○ The seller only under all circumstances

○ The buyer only under all circumstances

○ The lender only under all circumstances

What is the standard origination fee for the average loan amount?

○ 3%

○ 6%

○ 8%

○ 1%

A fraud detection system comprises which of the following?

○ A security guard

○ A database and operator

○ Doors and locks

○ Notary agents

What does the abbreviation CSBS mean?

○ Council of Statutory Business Supervisors

○ Conference of State Business Secretaries

○ Conference of State Bank Supervisors

○ Corporation of State Bank of Supervisors

Which of the following is true of a conventional conforming loan?

○ The federal government guarantees it.

○ The borrower must have a minimum FICO score of 620.

○ It must be an adjustable rate loan.

○ The borrower must make a down payment of at least 3%.

To which of the following does the term Subprime Mortgage Lending apply?

○ To all universities and their subsidiaries.

○ To Non- bank private finance organizations.

○ To all banks and their subsidiaries and bank holding companies and their nonbank subsidiaries.

○ To nonbank finance organizations and their subsidiaries

Which of the following statements is true?

○ The income cannot be derived from several sources.

○ The income can be derived from several sources, but it must be supported by historical documentation and have a high likelihood of continuation.

○ Determining the borrower's monthly income is an unimportant process.

○ Income derived from rental properties, interest, dividends, pensions and social security cannot be used.

How much will you pay if your per diem interest is 7.00% for $100,000 monthly?

○ $583.33 per month

○ $683.33 per month

○ $538.33 per month

○ $528.31 per month

The TILA requires full disclosure statements that outline all terms in simple easy-to-read language

○ Credit

○ Debit

○ Debt

○ Loss

Which of the following statements about business ethics is false?

○ Within a market economy, business behavior is independent from consumer behavior and consumer acceptance.

○ In the Internet age, such self-organization has become much easier, technologically and economically.

○ Business ethics as an academic field deals mainly with moral criticism (or self-criticism) of business behavior.

○ Business ethics should be more concerned with consumers and their behaviors

Which of the following statements is false?

○ The S.A.F.E. Act requires the agencies to jointly develop and maintain a system for registering residential mortgage loan originators.

○ The mortgage loan originators must be registered with the Nationwide Mortgage Licensing System and Registry.

○ The S.A.F.E. Act generally allows employees of an agency-regulated institution from originating residential mortgage loans without first registering with the Registry.

○ The proposal requires the mortgage loan originators to obtain a unique identifier through the Registry that will remain with the originator.

What is a conventional conforming loan?

○ Any mortgage that is not guaranteed or insured by the federal government.

○ The loan is a mortgage that meets the terms and conditions determined by Fannie Mae and Freddie Mac

○ A conventional conforming loan is a loan which is not government guaranteed, but which conforms to Fannie Mae/Freddie Mac requirements.

○ A loan that guaranteed by the federal government.

What is the meaning of "closing of loan" ?

○ Closing means the process of signing the loan documents and disbursing the loan funds.

○ Closing means the full repayment of the existing loan.

○ Closing of loan means the closure of the existing loan and sanctioning of an alternate loan.

○ Closing of loan means the closure of the existing loan forever.

What are "Borrower liabilities?

○ It is the amount remaining unpaid in his present borrower account.

○ It is the amount of installments due on a particular day.

○ It is the full loan amount sanctioned to him, whether some of the installments are paid or not.

○ The borrower's liabilities include all installment loans, revolving charge accounts, real estate loans, alimony, child support, and all other continuing obligations.

What does an FHA appraiser need not look for while appraising the value of your home?

○ The appraiser must check for required FHA items to insure that the property does not contain any health or safety issue.

○ Condition of the property at the time of purchase and if a home inspection report was obtained earlier.

○ The appraiser must typically use the 3-5 most recent sales within a 1 mile radius of the subject property,

○ The properties should be approximately the same size, with the same bedroom and bathroom count.

What is an example of an encumbrance on a title?

○ A lien.

○ An abstract.

○ A title flaw.

○ An escrow company.

When will your first mortgage repayment will be due if you are closing the earlier loan on January 19?

116

- On 19th of February
- On 1st of March
- On 19th of March
- On 1st of February

What is the expansion of TILA ?
- Trust In Lending Act
- Trust In Loan Act
- Truth In Lending Act
- Truth In Loan Act

The Real Estate Settlement Procedures Act (RESPA) is?
- A consumer protection statute covering residential mortgage loans
- A borrower protection statute covering residential mortgage loans
- A salesman protection statute covering residential mortgage loans
- An owner protection statute covering residential mortgage loans

**Notes:**

**Answers to National Component prep-test A**

TILA allows consumers _____ to back out of a loan transaction through a right of rescission.

- ○ 5 Business days
- ◉ 3 Business days
- ○ 7 Business days
- ○ 9 Business days

Fixed-Rate Conventional Mortgages are often referred to as?

- ○ 9 Business days
- ◉ 15-yr or 30-yr mortgage loans
- ○ 25-yr or 50-yr mortgage loans
- ○ 5-yr or 20-yr mortgage loans

What is a disadvantage of a Fixed-Rate Mortgage loan?

- ○ Interest rates are slightly lower than ARMs and other special mortgages
- ○ Interest rates are slightly lower than special mortgages
- ◉ Interest rates are usually slightly higher than ARMs and other special mortgages
- ○ ARMs are higher than Interest rates

Before a loan is ready to be underwritten, the following MUST be completed:

- ◉ Validated loan application, confirmation on the value of the property, and a title search
- ○ Validated loan application, monthly income confirmed, purchase of title
- ○ Evaluation of credit score, salary checked, debt obligations considered
- ○ Satisfactory down payment, evaluation of past and present loans, assurance of continued income

A title report does NOT include information on _____.

- ○ Property description
- ○ Tax rate
- ● Property history
- ○ Liens

Who ensures the accuracy of a title report?

- ● The insurance company
- ○ The title company
- ○ An abstractor attorney
- ○ An escrow company

If a lender charges a document preparation fee, where will it appear?

- ○ Direct Loan Costs section of the HUD-2
- ○ Loan Fees Costs section of the HUD-1.
- ○ Fees Costs section of the HUD-2
- ● Loan Fees/Direct Loan Costs section of the HUD-1

Which section of GLB Act prohibits the practice of accessing private information using false pretenses?

- ○ Safeguards Rule
- ● Pretexting Provisions
- ○ Privacy Provisions
- ○ Spoofing Provisions

What does BPO stand for?

- ○ Business Process Outside

○ Beneficiaries Payment Options

○ Brokers Price Option

◉ Brokers Price Opinions

Who is appointed temporarily under the revenue laws to value where there is no resident appraiser?

○ Any appraiser

○ A valuer

◉ Merchant appraiser

○ Resident appraiser

What does HCFP stand for?

○ Health and Community Facilities Programs

○ Housing and Community Facilities Projects

○ Housing and Commonality Facilities Programs

◉ Housing and Community Facilities Programs

Under HCFP who does the borrower work with directly?

○ Directly with the HCFP

◉ A private lender, such as a bank or credit union

○ A Federally appointed lender

○ Only a Credit Union certified by the HCFP

How many days does MDIA give to creditors to provide good faith estimates of mortgage loan costs?

◉ Three Business Days

○ Two Business Days

○ Five Business Days

○ Twenty Business Days

When was the Mortgage Disclosure Improvement Act enacted?

○ The Mortgage Disclosure Improvement Act enacted in July 2007

○ The Mortgage Disclosure Improvement Act enacted in July 2006

◉ The Mortgage Disclosure Improvement Act enacted in July 2008

○ The Mortgage Disclosure Improvement Act enacted in July 2005

If a borrower's rent payments are $1,000 per month and the borrower's total monthly income is $4,000. The PHE to Income Ratio is ___?

○ 28%

○ 20%

◉ 25%

○ 30%

In what instance would the closing agent open a new escrow account?

○ To cover the closing costs

○ To cover legal fees

○ Under no circumstances

◉ If the lender is covering the annual property taxes and insurance payments

What is the main purpose of FHA?

◉ To insure residential mortgage loans made by individual/private lenders

○ To set standards for construction

○ To set standards for underwriting

○ To provide loans to borrowers

A Conditional License issued to a salesperson may remain suspended for how many months for failing to submit transcripts?

- ○ 24
- ○ 36
- ◉ 18
- ○ 12

Morality appears to be _____ and _____ in nature

- ○ Subjective and intuitive
- ◉ Esoteric and qualitative
- ○ Learned and forgotten
- ○ Black and white

## Answers to National Component Test B

What does FFIEC stand for?

- ○ Federal Funding and Institutional Equity Capital
- ○ Future of Foreclosure and Integrated Equal Credit
- ○ Federal Fixed Insurance and Economy Control
- ◉ Federal Financial Institutions Examination Council

Which year was Truth in Lending Act Enacted?

- ◉ Truth in Lending Act Enacted in 1968
- ○ Truth in Lending Act Enacted in 1978
- ○ Truth in Lending Act Enacted in 1958
- ○ Truth in Lending Act Enacted in 1969

How do you determine your net worth?

○ Subtract the amount of your car loan from the resale value of your car.

○ Subtract your total credit card debt from the balance in your checking account.

◉ Subtract your total liabilities from your total assets.

○ Subtract your monthly taxes from your monthly income.

To find the index date, what should you refer to first?

○ Week and Time

◉ A multi-year calendar

○ Rate Change Worksheet

○ ARM's rate adjustment index

What are the three sections of Gramm-Leach-Bliley Act?

○ The three sections of Gramm-Leach-Bliley Act are: Privacy statement, Wealth disclosure statement and Re-funding statement.

○ The three sections of Gramm-Leach-Bliley Act are: Financial Modernization Act, Mortgage of assets Act and Regulatory Collection Act.

◉ The three sections of Gramm-Leach-Bliley Act are: Financial Privacy Rule, Safeguards Rule, and Pretexting provisions.

○ The three sections of Gramm-Leach-Bliley Act are: Prohibition of donations, Withdrawal of deposits and Payment of annual bonus.

Mortgage in itself is not a debt, but is a borrower's security for a loan?

○ A mortgage in itself is a debt; it is the lender's security for a debt.

◉ A mortgage in itself is not a debt; it is the lender's security for a debt.

○ A mortgage in itself is not a security; it is the borrower's debt for a loan.

○ A mortgage in itself is not a loan; it is the lender's debt for a security.

Who is an underwriter?

○ The borrower.

◉ A person who verifies the accuracy of mortgage documents

○ The guarantor, who guarantees mortgage.

○ A private lender

The Mortgage Disclosure Improvement Act (MDIA) seeks to inform consumers about....

◉ Estimated mortgage loan costs

○ Mortgage loans

○ Their credit history

○ Approximate mortgage fees

Does the buyer necessarily need to pay the premium for the lender's title insurance policy?

○ Yes

○ No, he never needs to pay for the lender's title insurance policy.

◉ No, not necessarily.

○ It depends on his choice.

Which of the following is the lender's responsibility?

○ Provide a comprehensive list of all the costs you may face.

○ Contact the buyer and arrange meeting times.

○ Email you when there is a suspected change in cost.

◉ Preparing estimate of costs you may incur when buying or refinancing

The lender collects and holds taxes in what type of account?

○ Savings

○ Checking

○ Trust

◉ Escrow

What reduces the amount of money that can be borrowed by most home buyers?

◉ Higher interest rates

○ Lower interest rates

○ Higher Mortgage Value

○ Lower Mortgage Value

What is the purpose of RESPA?

○ To protect lenders from unqualified borrowers

◉ To protect borrowers from improper lending practices

○ To make it easier to lend money

○ To keep lenders from having relationships with service providers

What does RESPA stand for?

○ Revolutionary Emerging Socialistic Pattern of Africa

○ Regional Enterprise Security Planning Act.

○ Regular Educational Service Program Act

◉ Real Estate Settlement and Procedures Act.

Who benefits from RESPA?

◉ Borrowers

○ Lender

○ Both Borrowers and Lenders

○ Neither Borrowers nor Lenders

Failure to submit transcripts will result in _____

○ A fine of $25.00

○ A delay in issuing the license

○ Being denied a license

◉ The automatic suspension of the conditional license

Name the two parts which makes the interest rate of ARM (Adjustable rate mortgage).

○ Cost and Income

◉ Index and Margin

○ Fixed and Variable

○ Variable and Margin

What is the extra amount which the lender adds to the index?

○ Cost of Fund Index

◉ Margin

○ An Interest-only (I-O) ARM

○ Settlement

How do you calculate the future value of investment in loan calculation?

◉ FV (rate, nper [, pmt] [, pv] [, type])

○ PV/ (pmt, rate)

○ FV (rate/PV, pmt, type)

○ PV (pmt/FV*pmt, type)

Which of the following statements about the 1003 Mortgage Application are true?

○ The 1003 Mortgage Application will generally list the borrower employment, unless the application is for a No Employment Verification Loan.

○ A 1003 Mortgage Application is the standard application filled out by a mortgage professional on behalf of a borrower applying for a mortgage loan.

○ Some lenders have the complete 1003 application on their websites.

◉ All of the statements are correct.

What is the purpose of a 1003 Mortgage application?

○ It is an application to apply for a mortgage to buy an industrial building.

○ It is an application to modify your mortgage payments.

◉ It is a verification application to help the lenders determine whether or not you will be able to pay off your mortgage

○ It is an application that you need to fill out if you are going to let someone assume your mortgage.

MDIA is the abbreviation for?

○ Mortgage Distribution Information Act

◉ Mortgage Disclosure Improvement Act

○ Monetary Digitization Information Act

○ Monthly Development Index Act

Which of the following factors does not determine the cost of home insurance?

◉ The details about the heirs of the owner.

○ How much value you insure your home for.

○ The age and condition of your property.

○ The location of your home (fire hydrant protection, quality of Fire Department, etc

Which of the following statements is not correct?

○ Hazard insurance is a generic term, referring to property insurance on your home.

127

○    Flood Insurance is available only through the National Flood Insurance Plan (NFIP).

○    Broader insurance coverage generally costs more than the lender required coverage.

◉    All of the above.


## Answers to National Component Test C
COE is an abbreviation for?

○    Cost of Eligibility

○    Certificate of Encumbrance

○    Certificate of Education

◉    Certificate Of Eligibility

Who is eligible for VA home loan benefits?

○    US military personnel

○    Honorably discharged veterans

○    active military

◉    All of the above

Who informs the buyer about the amount of funds to bring to the closing?

○    The insurance company

◉    The closing agent

○    The buyer's lender

○    The seller's agent

Which of the following statements is false?

○ The buyer's or borrower's main function at a closing is to review and sign the many documents related to the new mortgage, and to pay closing costs (if applicable to the transaction)

○ Some states have laws which require funding to occur 24-hours after closing

◉ In most states, the closing is conducted by attorneys in law offices.

○ A normal closing takes about one to two hours to complete

Closing costs may be paid by:

◉ The seller or the buyer

○ The seller only under all circumstances

○ The buyer only under all circumstances

○ The lender only under all circumstances

What is the standard origination fee for the average loan amount ?

○ 3%

○ 6%

○ 8%

◉ 1%

A fraud detection system comprises which of the following?

○ A security guard

◉ A database and operator

○ Doors and locks

○ Notary agents

What does the abbreviation CSBS mean?

○ Council of Statutory Business Supervisors

○ Conference of State Business Secretaries

○ Conference of State Bank Supervisors

○ Corporation of State Bank of Supervisors

Which of the following is true of a conventional conforming loan?

○ It is guaranteed by the federal government.

◉ The borrower must have a minimum FICO score of 620.

○ It must be an adjustable rate loan.

○ The borrower must make a down payment of at least 3%.

To which of the following does the term Subprime Mortgage Lending apply ?

○ To all universities and their subsidiaries.

○ To Non- bank private finance organizations.

◉ To all banks and their subsidiaries and bank holding companies and their nonbank subsidiaries.

○ To nonbank finance organizations and their subsidiaries

Which of the following statements is true?

○ The income cannot be derived from several sources.

◉ The income can be derived from several sources, but it must be supported by historical documentation and have a high likelihood of continuation.

○ Determining the borrower's monthly income is an unimportant process.

○ Income derived from rental properties, interest, dividends, pensions and social security cannot be used.

How much will you pay if your per deim interest is 7.00% for $100,000 monthly?

◉ $583.33 per month

○ $683.33 per month

○ $538.33 per month

○ $528.31 per month

The TILA requires full disclosure statements that outline all------terms in simple easy-to-read language

◉ credit

○ debit

○ debt

○ loss

Which of the following statements about business ethics is false?

◉ Within a market economy, business behavior is independent from consumer behavior and consumer acceptance.

○ In the Internet age, such self-organization has become much easier, technologically and economically.

○ Business ethics as an academic field deals mainly with moral criticism (or self-criticism) of business behavior.

○ Business ethics should be more concerned with consumers and their behaviors

Which of the following statements is false?

○ The S.A.F.E. Act requires the agencies to jointly develop and maintain a system for registering residential mortgage loan originators.

○ The mortgage loan originators must be registered with the Nationwide Mortgage Licensing System and Registry.

◉ The S.A.F.E. Act generally allows employees of an agency-regulated institution from originating residential mortgage loans without first registering with the Registry.

○ The proposal requires the mortgage loan originators to obtain a unique identifier through the Registry that will remain with the originator.

What is a conventional conforming loan?

○ Any mortgage that is not guaranteed or insured by the federal government.

○ The loan is a mortgage that meets the terms and conditions determined by Fannie Mae and Freddie Mac

◉ A conventional conforming loan is a loan which is not government guaranteed, but which conforms to Fannie Mae/Freddie Mac requirements.

○ A loan that guaranteed by the federal government.

What is the meaning of "closing of loan" ?

◉ Closing means the process of signing the loan documents and disbursing the loan funds.

○ Closing means the full repayment of the existing loan.

○ Closing of loan means the closure of the existing loan and sanctioning of an alternate loan.

○ Closing of loan means the closure of the existing loan forever.

What are "Borrower liabilities" ?

○ It is the amount remaining unpaid in his present borrower account.

○ It is the amount of installments due on a particular day.

○ It is the full loan amount sanctioned to him, whether some of the installments are paid or not.

◉ The borrower's liabilities include all installment loans, revolving charge accounts, real estate loans, alimony, child support, and all other continuing obligations.

What does an FHA appraiser need not look for while appraising the value of your home?

○ The appraiser must check for required FHA items to insure that the property does not contain any health or safety issue.

◉ Condition of the property at the time of purchase and if a home inspection report was obtained earlier.

○ The appraiser must typically use the 3-5 most recent sales within a 1 mile radius of the subject property,

○ The properties should be approximately the same size, with the same bedroom and bathroom count.

What is an example of an encumbrance on a title?

⦿ A lien.

○ An abstract.

○ A title flaw.

○ An escrow company.

When will your first mortgage repayment will be due if you are closing the earlier loan on January 19?

○ On 19th of February

⦿ On 1st of March

○ On 19th of March

○ On 1st of February

What is the expansion of TILA ?

○ Trust In Lending Act

○ Trust In Loan Act

⦿ Truth In Lending Act

○ Truth In Loan Act

The Real Estate Settlement Procedures Act (RESPA) is?

⦿ A consumer protection statute covering residential mortgage loans

○ A borrower protection statute covering residential mortgage loans

○ A salesman protection statute covering residential mortgage loans

○ An owner protection statute covering residential mortgage loans

## Mortgage Glossary

**1031 Exchange-** Refers to Section 1031 of the Internal Revenue Code, which authorizes investors to 'exchange' one investment property for another. This offers the investor some great tax advantages.

**Abstract (of title)-** A historical summary of all the recorded transactions that affect the title to the property. An attorney or a title company will review an abstract of title to determine if there are any problems affecting the title to the property. All such problems must be cleared before the buyer can be issued a clear and insurable title.

**Acceleration clause-** A loan provision giving the lender the power to declare all sums owing lender immediately due and payable upon the violation of a specific loan provision, such as the sale of the property, or the failure to make loan payments on time.

**Account termination fee-** A fee that is often charged if you pay in full and terminate your home equity line of credit during the first five years. Payment down to a zero balance usually does not count as termination. See also definition of prepayment penalty.

**Accretion-** The addition to land through natural forces like wind or water.

**Acknowledgment-** Formal declaration before a Notary Public or other public official that one has signed a document. Required before recording real estate legal documents, such as a deeds of trust.

**Acre-** 43,560 square feet of land.

**Additional principal payment-** A payment made by a borrower of more than the scheduled principal amount due, in order to reduce the outstanding balance on the loan, to save on interest over the life of the loan and/or pay off the loan early.

**Adjustable rate mortgage-** Mortgage where the interest rate changes periodically, usually in relation to an index, and payments may go up or down accordingly. The note rate equals the rate at the beginning of the loan.

**Adjustment date-** The date on which the interest rate changes for an adjustable-rate mortgage (ARM).

**Adjustment period-** The period that elapses between the adjustment dates for an adjustable rate mortgage (ARM), typically 6 months or 1 year.

**Affordability analysis-** A preliminary analysis of a borrower's ability to afford the purchase of a home. An affordability analysis takes into consideration factors such as income, liabilities, and available funds, along with the type of home loan, the likely taxes and insurance for the home, and the estimated closing costs.

**Agreement of sale-** Also known as contract of purchase, offer and acceptance, earnest money contract, or sales agreement.

**Amenity-** A feature of real property that enhances its attractiveness and increases the occupant's or user's satisfaction, although the feature is not essential to the property's use. Natural amenities include a pleasant or desirable location near water, scenic views, etc. Man-made amenities include swimming pools, tennis courts, community buildings, and other recreational facilities.

**Amortization-** The gradual repayment of a home loan by periodic installments.

**Amortization schedule-** A timetable for payment of a home loan. An amortization schedule shows the amount of each payment applied to interest and principal and the remaining balance after each payment is made.

**Amortization term-** The amount of time it takes to pay off the loan. The amortization term is expressed as a number of months. For example, for a 30 year fixed rate loan, the amortization term is 360 months.

**Amortize-** To repay a loan with regular payments that cover both principal and interest.

**Annual maintenance fee-** An amount that is charged each year for having a line of credit. It is charged regardless of whether or not the credit line is used. For some programs and in some states, an annual fee is not charged. The fee is usually waived the first year of the loan.

**Annual percentage rate-** A measure of the cost of credit, expressed as a yearly rate. It includes interest as well as other charges. Since all lenders follow the same rules to ensure the accuracy of the annual percentage rate, it provides borrowers with a good basis for comparing the cost of loans, including mortgage plans.

**Application-** A form to be completed by a home loan applicant with the lender's assistance to provide pertinent information about a prospective borrower's employment, income, assets, debts and other financial information, about the purpose of the home loan, and about the property securing the home loan. Lenders also sometimes call it a 1003 (ten o three) the form number of Fannie Mae's standard application form.

**Application fee-** A fee usually paid at the time an application is given to a lender for helping to complete and review an application. Some lenders collect fees for a property appraisal and a credit report, instead of an application fee, at the time of application.

**Appraisal-** A written analysis or opinion of the estimated value of a property prepared by a qualified appraiser. Contrast with home inspection.

**Appraised value-** The dollar figure for a property's estimated fair market value, based on an appraiser's knowledge, experience, and analysis of the property and comparable properties near by.

**Appraiser-** A person qualified by education, training, experience, and state licensure to estimate the value of real property.

**Appreciation-** An increase in the value of a property due to changes in market conditions or other causes. Inflation, increased demand, home improvement, and sweat equity are all causes of appreciation.

**Arm's length transaction-** A transaction where all parties involved acts in his or her own best interest. Most deals between family members, especially parents and children, are not arms length. This is because people have been known to cut family members a break in price.

**Assessed value-** The value used to determine property taxes, based on a public tax assessor's opinion. Contrast with appraised value.

**Assessment-** The amount of tax due to local government. May also refer to the amount due to local government or to common owners of a property (e.g., a homeowner's association) for a special payment to cover expenses for improvements or maintenance, such as new sewers or roads.

**Assessment rolls-** A public record of the assessed value of property in the taxing jurisdiction.

**Assessor-** A public official who establishes the value of a property for taxation purposes.

**Asset (1)-** Anything of monetary value that is owned by a person. Assets include real property, personal property, and enforceable claims against others (including bank accounts, stocks, mutual funds, and so on). (2) Anything that produces a regular positive cash flow.

**Assignment-** The method of transferring a right or contract, such as the terms of a loan, from one person to another.

**Assumability-** When a home is sold, the seller may be able to transfer the mortgage to the new buyer. This means the mortgage is assumable. Lenders generally require a credit review of the new borrower and may charge a fee for the assumption. Some mortgages contain a Due on Sale clause, which means that the mortgage may not be transferable to a new buyer. Instead, the lender may make the borrower pay the entire balance that is due when the some is sold. Assumability can help the seller attract buyers when he/she sells his/her home.

**Assumable loan-** A home loan that allows a new purchaser of the home to take over ("assume") the loan obligations of the seller when a home is sold.

**Assumption-** The buyer's acceptance of liability for the seller's existing home loan.

**Assumption clause-** A provision in an assumable loan that allows a buyer to assume responsibility for the home loan from the seller. The loan does not need to be paid in full by the original borrower (seller) upon sale or transfer of the property.

**Assumption fee-** The fee paid to a lender (usually by the buyer) for the lender's agreement to start collecting payment from the buyer instead of the original borrower (seller).

**Attorney in fact-** One who is authorized to act for another under a power of attorney, which may be general or limited in scope. For example: Bob is in the process of selling his house when his job requires him to be out of state during the week of the closing. So Bob authorizes George to sign the grant deed to sell the property to the buyer. With the proper paperwork completed, George becomes Bob's Attorney In Fact.

**Balance sheet-** A financial statement that shows an individual's assets, liabilities, and net worth as of a specific date.

**Balloon loan-** A loan that has level monthly payments that will amortize it over a stated term (e.g., 30 years) but that requires a lump sum payment of the entire principal balance at the end of a shorter term (e.g., 10 years).

**Balloon payment-** The final lump sum payment that is made at the end of the shorter term for a balloon loan and pays the loan in full.

**Bankrupt-** A person, firm, or corporation that is financially unable to pay debts when due. The debtor seeks relief through a court proceeding to work out a payment schedule or erase debts. In some cases, the debtor must surrender control of all assets to a court-appointed trustee.

**Bankruptcy-** A proceeding in a federal court in which a debtor who is financially unable to pay debts when due seeks relief to work out a payment schedule or erase debts.

**Basis point-** A basis point is equal to one one-hundredth of one percent (1/100 x .01%) or one one-hundredth of one point. For example: 5.76% is one basis point higher than 5.75%.

**Beneficiary-** The person who receives or is to receive the benefits resulting from certain acts.

**Biweekly payment loan-** A loan that requires payments to reduce the debt every two weeks (instead of the standard monthly payment schedule). The 26 (or possibly 27) biweekly payments are each equal to one-half of the monthly payment that would be required if the loan were a standard 30 year fixed rate loan, and they are usually drafted from the borrower's bank account. the lender.

**Borrower-** One who borrows money or, in hopes of borrowing money, applies for a loan.

**Breach-** A violation of terms of any legal obligation.

**Bridge loan-** A type of mortgage financing between the termination of one loan and the start of another loan.

**Budget-** A detailed plan of income and expenses expected over a certain period of time. A budget can provide guidelines for managing future investments and expenses.

**Building code-** Local regulations that specify minimum structural requirements for design of, construction of, and materials used in a home or office building. Building codes are based on safety and health standards.

**Buy down-** A temporary buy down gives a borrower a reduced monthly payment during the first few years of a home loan and is typically paid for in an initial lump sum made by the seller, lender, or borrower. A permanent buy down is paid the same way but reduces the interest rate over the entire life of a home loan.

**Buy down account-** An account in which funds are held so that they can be applied as part of the monthly loan payment as each payment comes due during the period that an interest rate buy down plan is in effect.

**Buyer's agent-** An agent hired by a buyer to locate a property for purchase. The agent represents the buyer and negotiates with the seller's agent for the best possible deal for the buyer.

**Buyers market-** Market conditions that favor buyers i.e. there are more sellers than buyers in the market. As a result buyers have ample choice of properties and may negotiate lower prices.

**Call option-** A provision in a loan that gives the lender the right to accelerate the debt, and require for full payment of the loan immediately, at the end of a specified period or for specified reason.

**Cap-** A provision of an adjustable-rate mortgage (ARM) that limits how much the interest rate or loan payments may increase or decrease. In upward rate markets, it protects the borrower from large increases in the interest rate or monthly payment. See lifetime payment cap, lifetime rate cap, periodic payment cap, and periodic rate cap.

**Capacity utilization-** The capacity utilization rate measures the percent of industrial output currently in use. A change in the rate indicates a change in the direction of economic activity.

**Capital improvement-** Any structure or component erected as a permanent improvement to real property that adds to its value and useful life.

**Cash available for closing-** Borrower funds available to cover down payment and closing costs. If lending guidelines require the borrower to have cash reserves at the time the loan closes or that the down payment come from certain sources, borrower's cash available for closing does not include cash reserves or money from other sources.

**Cash flow-** The flow, or direction of your money. Cash coming in is income and cash going out is expense. Individual items are classified as an income, expense, asset or liability based on the direction the cash flows.

**Cash-out refinance-** A refinance transaction in which the new loan amount exceeds the total of the principal balance of the existing first mortgage and any secondary mortgages or liens, together with closing costs and points for the new loan. This excess is usually given to the borrower in cash and can often be used for debt consolidation, home improvement, or any other purpose.

**Ceiling-** The maximum interest rate that can accrue on a variable rate loan or adjustable rate mortgage. See also: lifetime rate cap

**Certificate of Eligibility COE-** The document issued by the Veterans Administration to those that qualify for a VA loan. Certificates of eligibility may be obtained by sending the form DD-214 to the local VA office along with VA form 1880.

**Certificate of Occupancy-** A document issued by a local governmental agency stating a property meets the local building standards for occupancy, public health, and building codes. Some lenders require this documentation prior to closing a loan on a residential property.

**Certificate of reasonable value-** abr. CRV A document issued by the Department of Veterans Affairs (VA) that establishes the maximum value and loan amount for a VA loan, based on an approved appraisal.

**Certificate of Title-** A document provided by an attorney or licensed closing agent giving the status of title to a property, according to the public records. This certificate does not provide the same level of protection as title insurance. Some times, title companies will issue both certificate of title and title insurance.

**Chain of title-** The chronological order of conveyance of a parcel of land from the original owner (usually the US government) to the present owner. Many times, lenders will require a 6 or 12-month chain. In such a case the lender is looking to see that the same person has owned the property for the entire time.

**Clear title-** A marketable title, free of liens, clouds and disputed interests. Most lenders require a clear title prior to closing. Title insurance guarantee a clear title, otherwise the insurance policy will cover any costs involved in clearing the title up to repaying owner for costs involved in purchasing the property.

**Closing-** A meeting at which all documents are signed and all expenses are paid to transfer ownership of property. Also called "settlement A fee or amount that a home buyer must pay at closing for a particular service, tax, or product. Closing costs are made up of individual closing cost items such as origination fees and attorney's fees. Many closing cost items are included as numbered items on the HUD-1 settlement statement.

**Closing costs-** Various expenses (over and above the price of the property) incurred by buyers and sellers in transferring ownership of a property. Closing costs normally include items such as broker's commissions; discount points, origination fees, attorney's fees, taxes, title insurance premiums, escrow agent fees, and charges for obtaining appraisals, inspections and surveys. Closing costs will vary according to the area of the country. Lenders or real estate professionals often provide estimates of closing costs to prospective homebuyers even before the HUD-1 settlement statement is delivered.

**Closing statement-** An accounting of funds given to both buyer and seller before real estate is sold. See HUD-1 settlement statement.

**Cloud on title-** An outstanding claim or lien, revealed by a title search, that adversely affects the owner's title to real estate. Usually, clouds on title cannot be removed except by a quitclaim deed, release, or court action. Lenders usually require clouds to be fixed before closing.

**Co-op-** Co-op, or cooperative, is an apartment building or a group of dwellings owned by a corporation whose stockholders are the residents of the dwellings. It is operated for their benefit by their elected board of directors. In a cooperative, the corporation or association owns title to the real estate.

**Co-signer-** A person who signs a promissory note along with the borrower. A co-maker's signature helps to assure that the loan will be repaid. The borrower and the co-maker are jointly responsible for the repayment of the loan.

**Coinsurance-** A sharing of insurance risk between the insurer and the insured. Coinsurance depends on the relationship between the amount of the policy and a specified percentage of the actual value of the property insured at the time of the loss.

**Coinsurance clause-** A provision in a hazard insurance policy stating the minimum amount of coverage that must be maintained - as a percentage of the total value of the property - in order for the insured to collect the full amount of a loss.

**Collateral-** An asset (such as a car or a home) that is pledged as security for the repayment of a loan. The borrower risks losing the asset if the loan is not repaid according to the terms of the loan contract or promissory note.

**Collection-** The efforts used to bring a delinquent loan current and, if necessary, to file legal papers and notices to proceed with foreclosure.

**Combined loan to value-** abr. CLTV The ratio of the total amount borrowed on all mortgages against a property compared to the appraised value of the property. For example, if you have an $80,000 1st mortgage and a $10,000 2nd mortgage on a home with an appraised value of $100,000, the CLTV is 90% ($80,000+$10,000 = $90,000 / $100,000 = 90%).

**Commission-** The fee charged by a broker or agent for negotiating a real estate or loan transaction. A commission is generally a percentage of the price of the property or loan (such as 3%, 5%, or 6%).

**Commitment letter-** A formal notification from a lender stating that the borrower's loan has been conditionally approved and specifying the terms under which lender agrees make the loan. Also known as a "loan commitment.

**Common area assessments-** Payments required of individual unit owners in a condominium or planned unit development (PUD) project for additional capital to defray homeowners' association costs and expenses and to repair, replace, maintain, improve, or operate the common areas of the project.

**Common areas-** Those portions of a building, land, and amenities owned (or managed) by a planned unit development (PUD) or condominium project's homeowners' association (or a cooperative project's cooperative corporation) that are used by all of the unit owners, who share in the common expenses of their operation and maintenance. Common areas include swimming pools, tennis courts, and other recreational facilities, as well as common corridors of buildings, parking areas, means of ingress and egress, etc.

**Community property-** In some Western and Southwestern states, the law specifies that property acquired during a marriage is presumed to be owned jointly by the husband and wife unless acquired as separate property of one spouse or the other.

**Comparables-** abr. comps An abbreviation for "comparable properties"; used for comparative purposes in the appraisal process. Comparables are properties like the property under consideration; they have reasonably the same size, location, and amenities and have recently been sold. Comparables help the appraiser determine the approximate fair market value of the subject property. Syn: comps, comparable properties

**Compound interest-** Interest paid on the principal balance and on the accrued and unpaid interest. -

**Condemnation-** (1) Declaration that a building is unfit for use or is dangerous and must be destroyed; (2) taking of private property for a public use (such as a park, street or school) through an exercise of the right of eminent domain.

**Conditional commitment-** A written document provided by a lender agreeing to loan money provided certain conditions are met prior to closing.

**Condominium-** A real estate project in which each unit owner has title to a unit in a multi-unit building, an undivided interest in the common areas of the project, and sometimes the exclusive use of certain limited common areas.

**Conforming loan-** A home loan with a maximum loan amount that is eligible for purchase by FNMA and FHLMC.

**Consolidation loan-** A consolidation loan combines several student loans into one bigger loan from a single lender. The consolidation loan is used to pay off the balances on the other loans.

**Construction loan-** A short-term, interim loan for financing the cost of home construction. The lender makes payments to the builder at periodic intervals as the work progresses.

**Consumer reporting agency-** An organization that prepares reports that lenders use to determine a potential borrower's credit history. The agency obtains data for these reports from a credit repository as well as from creditors such as mortgage lenders, credit card companies, department stores, etc. Syn: consumer reporting bureau

**Contingency-** A condition that must be met before a contract is legally binding. For example, home purchasers often include a contingency that specifies that the contract is not binding until the purchaser obtains a satisfactory home inspection report from a qualified home inspector.

**Contract-** An oral or written agreement to do or not do something.

**Contract rate-** The rate of interest charged on the re-payment of a loan during the duration of the re-payment.

**Conventional loan-** A home loan that is not insured or guaranteed by the federal government. Contrast with government loan. Can be for conforming or non-conforming loan amounts.

**Conversion-** The borrower's agreement with the lender can have a clause that lets the borrower convert an ARM to a Fixed Rate Mortgage at designated times. When converted, the new rate is generally set at the current market rate for Fixed Rate Mortgages.

**Conversion clause-** A provision in some ARMs that allows the borrower to change the ARM to a fixed rate loan at some point during the term. Usually, conversion is allowed at the end of the first adjustment period. At the time of the conversion, the now fixed rate is generally set at one of the rates then prevailing for Fixed Rate Mortgages. The conversion feature may be available at an extra

**Convertibility clause-** A provision in some adjustable rate mortgages (ARM) that allows the borrower to change the ARM to a fixed rate loan at specified times during the life of the loan.

**Convertible ARM-** An adjustable rate mortgage (ARM) that can be converted to a fixed rate loan under specified conditions.

**Conveyance-** The transfer of title of real property from one party to another.

**Cooperative-** abr. co-op A type of multiple ownership in which the residents of a multi-unit housing complex own shares in the cooperative corporation that owns the property, giving each resident the right to occupy a specific apartment or unit.

**Cost of funds index-** abbr. COFI An index that is used to determine interest rate changes for certain adjustable-rate mortgage (ARM) plans. It represents the weighted-average cost of savings, borrowings, and advances of the 11th District members of the Federal Home Loan Bank of San Francisco. Syn: â–ºCOFI

**Covenant-** A promise in a mortgage or deed that requires or prevents certain uses of the property that, if violated, may result in loss or foreclosure of the property.

**Credit-** An agreement in which a borrower receives money or something of value in exchange for a promise to repay the lender on specified terms at a later time.

**Credit history-** An evaluation of an individual's capacity and history of debt repayment. A credit history helps a lender to determine whether a potential borrower is likely to repay a loan in a timely manner.

**Credit life insurance-** A type of insurance that pays off a loan if one of the borrowers dies while the policy is in force.

**Credit limit-** The maximum amount that can be borrowed under the home equity line of credit.

**Credit rating-** An expression of creditworthiness based upon present financial condition and past credit history.

**Credit report-** A report of an individual's credit history prepared by a credit bureau and used by a lender in determining a loan applicant's credit worthiness.

**Credit repository-** An organization that gathers, records, updates, and stores financial and public records information about the payment records of individuals who are being considered for credit. Syn: credit bureau

**Credit scores-** Credit scores are numerical values that rank individuals according to their credit history at a given point in time. Your score is based on your past payment history, the amount of credit you have outstanding, the amount of credit you have available, and other factors. According to Fannie Mae one of the major investors in home loans, credit scores have proven to be very good predictors of whether a borrower will repay his or her loan. To get a copy of your credit score, check out the services offered by myFICO.com or Credit Karma.com

**Creditor-** A person to whom money is owed.

**CRV-** a CRV (Certificate of Reasonable Value) is just an appraisal that's performed by an appraiser who is VA approved. Similar to a regular appraisal, it establishes the property's current market value and thus the maximum VA mortgage loan amount.

**Cumulative interest-** Total interest accrued.

**Curtailment-** A payment that reduces the principal balance of a loan.

**Debt-** An amount owed to another.

**Deed-** The legal document conveying title to a property.

**Deed of trust-** The document used in some states instead of a mortgage; title is vested in a trustee to secure repayment of the loan.

**Deed restriction-** A clause in a deed that limits the use of the property. Common deed restrictions are things such as, no house can be build, no businesses, or even something like, a road cannot be built on the land.

**Deed-in-lieu-** A deed given by a borrower to the lender to satisfy a debt and avoid foreclosure. Also called a "voluntary conveyance.

**Default-** Failure to make loan payments on a timely basis or to comply with other requirements of a mortgage.

**Defective title-** Any recorded instrument (liens or encumbrances) that would prevent a grantor/seller from giving a clear title.

**Deficiency judgment-** Personal claim against the debtor when the sale of foreclosed property does not yield sufficient proceeds to pay off the mortgages, accrued interest, legal fees, etc.

**Delinquency-** Failure to make mortgage payments when due.

**Department of Veterans Affairs-** An agency of the federal government that guarantees residential mortgages made to eligible veterans of the military services. The guarantee protects the lender against loss and thus encourages lenders to make mortgages to veterans.

**Deposit-** A sum of money given to bind the sale of real estate, or a sum of money given to ensure payment or an advance of funds in the processing of a loan. See also: earnest money deposit

**Depreciation-** A decline in the value of property because of physical or economic changes such as wear and tear; the opposite of appreciation.

**Discount-** Some lenders offer initial rates on ARMs and Fixed Rate Mortgages that are lower than other current rates. Such rates, called Discounted Rates, are often combined with large initial loan fees (Discount Points). These discounted rates are also known as buy downs.

**Discount points-** Amounts paid to the lender at origination to lower the rate on the face of the note.

**Documentary tax stamps-** Stamps affixed to a deed showing the amount of transfer tax paid upon the last conveyance.

**Dower-** The rights of a widow or child to part of a deceased husband or father's property.

**Down payment-** The part of the purchase price of a property that the buyer pays in cash and does not finance with a home loan.

**Dragnet clause-** A provision in a mortgage that pledges several properties as collateral. A default in the mortgage could lead to foreclosure proceedings on any of the properties in the dragnet.

**Draw period-** The time period in which the borrower may access and use a line of credit.

**Due-on-sale provision-** A provision in a mortgage home loan that allows the lender to demand repayment in full if the borrower sells the property that serves as security for the loan.

**Due-on-transfer provision-** This terminology is usually used for second mortgages.

**Earnest money-** A deposit made by the potential homebuyer to show that he or she is serious about buying the house.

**Easement-** A right of way giving to persons other than the owner to access to or over a property.

**Effective age-** An appraiser's estimate of the physical condition of a building. The actual age of a building may be shorter or longer than its effective age.

**Effective gross income-** A borrowers normal annual income, including overtime that is regular or guaranteed. Salary is usually the principal source, but other income may qualify if it is significant and stable.

**Encumbrance-** Anything that affects or limits the fee simple title to a property, such as mortgages, leases, easements, deeds, or restrictions.

**Endorser-** A person who signs a check or promissory note over to another party. Contrast with co-signer.

**Equal Credit Opportunity Act-** abbr. ECOA A federal law that requires lenders and other creditors to make credit equally available without discrimination based on race, color, religion, national origin, age, sex, marital status, or receipt of income from public assistance programs.

**Equity-** A homeowner's financial interest in a property. Equity is the difference between the fair market value of the property and the amount still owed on any home loans or liens against the property.

**Equity sharing-** Equity sharing is where the occupant and the investor share an interest in a property. This is usually done for tax advantages available to both parties. Upon sale of the property the owners split, or share, the profits based on the percentage ownership they hold.

**Escheat-** Escheat is the reversion of property back to the state in cases where the owner dies without leaving a will or legal heirs.

**Escrow-** An item of value, money, or documents deposited with a third party to be delivered upon the fulfillment of a condition.

**Escrow account-** The account in which a loan servicer holds the borrower's escrow payments prior to paying property expenses, such as property taxes or homeowners insurance.

**Escrow analysis-** The periodic examination of escrow accounts to determine if current monthly deposits will provide sufficient funds to pay taxes, insurance, and other bills when due.

**Escrow collections-** Funds collected by the loan servicer and set aside in an escrow account to pay borrower expenses such as property taxes, mortgage insurance, and hazard homeowners insurance.

**Escrow disbursements-** The use of escrow funds to pay real estate taxes, homeowners insurance, mortgage insurance, and other property expenses as they become due.

**Escrow payment-** The portion of a borrower's monthly payment that is held by the loan servicer to pay for taxes, hazard homeowners insurance, mortgage insurance, lease payments, and other items as they become due. Known as "impounds" or "reserves" in some states.

**Estate-** The ownership interest of an individual in real property. The sum total of all the real property and personal property owned by an individual at time of death.

**Eviction-** A legal proceeding by a landlord to recover possession of real property from the tenant.

**Examination of title-** The report on the title of a property from the public records or an abstract of the title.

**Executor-** An executor, or executrix for the ladies, is a person named in a will to carry out the provisions of said will.

**Farmer's Home Administration-** Farmer's Home Administration (FHA) is an agency of the federal government that provides credit assistance to farmers and other individuals who live in rural areas.

**Federal Home Loan Mortgage Corporation-** Federal Home Loan Mortgage Corporation (FHLMC, Freddie Mac) is a corporation authorized by Congress to provide a secondary market for residential mortgages. In addition, Freddie Mac also works with mortgage lenders to help people get lower housing costs and better access to home financing.

**Federal Housing Administration-** The Federal Housing Administration (FHA) is the federal agency in the Department of Housing and Urban Development that insures residential mortgages in an effort to provide affordable mortgages everyone.

**Federal National Mortgage Association-** The Federal National Mortgage Association (FNMA, Fannie Mae) is a federally chartered corporation that purchases mortgage loans from lenders.

**Finance charge-** A fee charged (interest) by the issuer of a lender or credit card company. The fee for borrowing money.

**First mortgage-** A mortgage that has priority as a lien over all other mortgages. In the case of a foreclosure the first mortgage will be satisfied before other mortgages.

**Fixture-** Improvements or personal property attached to the land so as to become a part of the real estate. Fixtures are transferred to the buyer upon sale of the property. When in doubt if something is a fixture, make sure to clarify it in the sales contract.

**Flood insurance-** An insurance policy that covers property damage due to natural flooding. Flood insurance may be required on properties in a flood zone. Be advised that most standard home insurance policies don't include flood coverage.

**Foreclosure-** A legal process by which the lender takes possession of a property because the borrower has not met the terms of the loan agreement. Houses are usually then auctioned off.

**FSBO-** A property that is "for sale by owner". Many people sell their houses this way to keep from having to pay a real estate agent commissions.

**General warranty deed-** A deed that not only conveys all of the grantor's interests in the property, but also warrants that if the title is defective or has a cloud (such as mortgage claims, tax liens, title claims, judgments, or mechanic's liens against it), the grantee may hold the grantor liable. Used in most real estate deed transfers, a general warranty deed offers the greatest protection of any deed.

**Government loan-** A loan that is insured by the Federal Housing Administration (FHA) or guaranteed by the Department of Veterans Affairs (VA) or the Rural Housing Service (RHS). Contrast with conventional loan.

**Government National Mortgage Association-** The Government National Mortgage Association (also known as GNMA and Ginnie Mae) is an owned government association.

**Graduated payment mortgage-** A GPM is a mortgage that has lower payments initially which increase each year until the loan is fully amortized. GPM's sometimes have a negative amortization at the beginning until the payment rises.

**Grandfather clause-** An exemption based on circumstances existing prior to the adoption of some policy. In the mortgage arena this is usually dealt with in the area of city zoning, where an containing houses is zoned commercial or industrial. The city doesn't force the residents to leave - they grandfather them in.

**Grantee-** The person to whom an interest in real property is conveyed (e.g. the buyer).

**Grantor-** The person who conveys an interest in real property (e.g. the seller).

**Gross monthly income-** Normal annual income including overtime that is regular or guaranteed. The before taxes income may be from more than one source. Salary is generally the principal source, but other income may qualify if it is significant and stable.

**Ground rent-** The amount of money that is paid for the use of land when title to a property is held as a leasehold estate rather than as a fee simple estate.

**Group home-** A single-family residential structure designed or adapted for occupancy by unrelated developmentally disabled persons. The structure provides long-term housing and support services that are residential in nature.

**Hazard insurance-** Hazard Insurance, also known as fire insurance or homeowners insurance, is insurance on a property against fire and other risks. The policy will usually have additional coverage for theft, liability, etc that a fire insurance policy may not cover. Note, that these policies rarely, if ever, cover flood damage.

**Home equity line of credit-** abbr. HELOC - A mortgage loan, which is usually in a subordinate position, that allows the borrower to obtain multiple advances of the loan proceeds at his or her own discretion, up to an amount that represents a specified percentage of the borrower's equity in a property.

**Home inspection-** A thorough inspection that evaluates the structural and mechanical condition of a property. A satisfactory home inspection is often included as a contingency by the purchaser. Contrast with appraisal.

**Homeowner's warranty-** A type of insurance that covers repairs to specified parts of a house for a specific period of time. The builder or property seller as a condition of the sale may provide it but homeowners can also purchase it.

**Homeowner's association-** A nonprofit association that manages the common areas of a planned unit development (PUD) or condominium project. In a condominium project, it has no ownership interest in the common elements. In a PUD project, it holds title to the common elements. See also master association. See also: planned unit development

**Homestead- 1)** the home and adjacent grounds occupied by a family 2) land acquired from the United States public lands by filing a record and living on and cultivating it under the homestead law 3) dwelling that is usually a farmhouse and adjoining land 4) a legal classification of a house used to protect ones home from creditors (may not be available in all states).

**Homestead exemption-** Available in some states - this causes the assessed value of a principal residence to be reduced by the amount of the exemption for the purposes of calculating property tax.

**Housing code-** A set of local government ordinances that set minimum standards of safety and sanitation for existing residential buildings.

**Housing expense ratio -** The percentage of gross monthly income that goes toward paying housing expenses.

**HUD-** Department of Housing and Urban Development is the United States federal department that administers federal programs dealing with better housing and urban renewal. FHA is part of HUD.

**HUD median income-** Median family income for a particular county or metropolitan statistical area (MSA), as estimated by the Department of Housing and Urban Development (HUD).

**HUD-1 settlement statement-** A document that provides an itemized listing of the funds that are payable at closing. Items that appear on the statement include real estate commissions, loan fees, points, and initial escrow amounts. A separate number within a standardized numbering system represents each item on the statement. The totals at the bottom of the HUD-1 statement define the seller's net proceeds and the buyer's net payment at closing. The blank form for the statement is published by the Department of Housing and Urban Development (HUD). The HUD-1 statement is also known as the "closing statement" or "settlement sheet. .

**Hypothecate-** to pledge without delivery or title of possession

**Impound account-** That portion of a borrower's monthly payments held by the lender or servicer to pay for taxes, hazard insurance, mortgage insurance, lease payments, and other items as they become due. Also known as reserves.

**In-file credit report-** An objective account, normally computer-generated, of credit and other financial information obtained from a credit-reporting agency.

**Income approach-** A method used by an appraiser to estimate the value of a property based on the income it generates.

**Income property-** Real estate developed, purchased, or improved for the purpose of producing income.

**Ingress-** the act of entering a property.

**Initial draw amount-** The amount of the home equity line of credit that the borrower is requesting at closing (up to, but never exceeding, the credit line amount).

**Initial interest rate-** The starting interest rate for an adjustable-rate mortgage (ARM) loan or variable-rate home equity line of credit. At the end of the effective period for the initial rate, the interest rate adjusts periodically during the life of the loan based on changes in a specified financial index. Sometimes known as "start rate," "intro rate" or "teaser rate

**Installment loan-** Borrowed money that is repaid in equal payments, known as installments. A furniture loan is often paid for as an installment loan.

**Insurable title-** A property title that a title insurance company agrees to insure against defects and disputes.

**Insurance-** A contract that provides compensation for specific losses in exchange for a periodic payment. An individual contract is known as an insurance policy, and the periodic payment is known as an insurance premium.

**Insured mortgage-** A mortgage that is protected by the Federal Housing Administration (FHA) or by private mortgage insurance (PMI). If the borrower defaults on the loan, the insurer must pay the lender the lesser of the loss incurred or the insured amount.

**Interest-** The fee charged for borrowing money.

**Interest accrual rate-** The percentage rate at which interest accrues on the mortgage. In most cases, it is also the rate used to calculate the monthly payments.

**Interest payment-** The portion of a monthly payment that goes to interest based on the amortization schedule.

**Interest rate-** The percentage rate of return charged for use of a sum of money. This percentage rate is specified in the mortgage note. See note rate.

**Interest rate buy down-** A temporary buy down gives a borrower a reduced monthly payment during the first few years of a home loan and is typically paid for in an initial lump sum made by the seller, lender, or borrower. A permanent buy down is paid the same way but reduces the interest rate over the entire life of a home loan.

**Interest rate caps-** An Interest Rate Cap places a limit on the amount your interest rate can increase. Interest caps come in two versions: * Periodic Caps - which limit the interest rate, increase from one adjustment period to the next.

**Introductory rate-** The starting rate for a home equity loan, line of credit or adjustable-rate mortgage, usually a discounted rate, for a short period of time.

**Investment property-** A property that is not occupied by the owner and is generally rented to a tenant to produce income.

**Joint and several liabilities-** A type of liability shared by two or more people, which is divisible. A creditor can demand full repayment from any and/or all of those who share in the liability. Each borrower is individually liable for the full debt, not just the prorated share. Joint and several liabilities has been the subject of much legal reform.

**Joint tenancy-** A form of co-ownership that gives each tenant equal undivided interest and rights in the property, including the right of survivorship. Contrast with tenancy in common, tenancy by the entirety.

**Judgment-** A decree by a court of law that one person, a debtor, is indebted to another, a creditor, in a specified amount. The court may place a lien against the debtor's real property as collateral for payment of the judgment to the creditor.

**Judgment lien-** A lien on the property of a debtor resulting from a judgment.

**Judicial foreclosure-** A type of foreclosure proceeding used in some states that is handled as a civil lawsuit where the court confirms the sales price for the property and the distribution of the sale proceeds.

**Jumbo loan -**A loan that exceeds Fannie Mae's legislated mortgage amount limits of $300,700. Also called a nonconforming loan.

**Kicker-** A payment required by a mortgage in addition to normal principal and interest. Sometimes known as a participation loan.

**Land contract-** A real estate contract that allows the buyer to use and occupy the property, but no deed is given by seller until the sales price has been paid in full.

**Late charge-** The penalty a borrower must pay when a payment is made a stated number of days (usually 10-15) after the due date.

**Lease-** A written agreement between the property owner and a tenant that stipulates the conditions under which the tenant may use the real estate for a specified period of time and the amount of rent to be paid.

**Lease with option to purchase-** A lease under which the lessee has the right to purchase the property. The option may run for a portion or for the full length of the lease. It's usually best to include items such as sales price and down payment amount in the lease at the time of signing.

**Leasehold estate-** A tenant's interest in or right to hold possession of a property.

**Legal description-** A property description, recognized by law, using a government rectangular survey, metes and bounds, or a plat map to sufficiently locate and identify a property.

**Lender's fees-** Fees paid to the lender to cover costs associated with processing, underwriting and closing of the loan.

**Lessee-** A person who leases a property.

**Lessor-** A person whom others lease property from.
**Liabilities-** A person's debts or financial obligations. Liabilities include long-term and short-term debt, as well as potential losses from legal claims.

**Liability insurance-** Insurance coverage that offers protection against claims alleging that a property owner's negligence or inappropriate action resulted in bodily injury or property damage to another party. See also homeowners insurance.

**Lien-** A legal claim against a property that must be paid off when the property is sold. A lien is created when you borrow money to purchase or refinance a home loan or and with obtain a home equity loan.

**Lifetime rate cap-** For an adjustable-rate mortgage (ARM), a limit on the amount that the interest rate can increase or decrease over the life of the loan.

**Line amount-** The entire HELOC or Fixed Rate Second mortgage loan amount.

**Liquid asset-** A cash asset or an asset that is easily converted into cash.
**Loan amount** -A sum of borrowed money (principal) that is generally repaid over time with interest.

**Loan commitment-** A lender's agreement to advance money on specified terms after specified conditions are met.

**Loan origination-** The process by which a mortgage lender makes a home loan and records a mortgage against the borrower's real property as security for repayment of the loan.

**Loan-to-value-** abbr. LTV The ratio of the total amount borrowed on a mortgage against a property compared to the appraised value of the property. For example, if you have an

$80,000 1st mortgage on a home with an appraised value of $100,000, the LTV is 80% ($80,000 / $100,000 = 80%).

**Lock-in-** A written agreement in which the lender guarantees a specified loan program interest rate and points if a mortgage goes to closing within a set period of time.

**Lock-in period-** The time period during which the lender has guaranteed an interest rate to a borrower.

**Margin-** For an adjustable-rate mortgage (ARM) or home equity line of credit, the amount that is added to the index to establish the interest rate on each adjustment date, subject to any limitations on the interest rate change. The margin is static and will not change during the life of the loan.

**Market value-** The highest price that a buyer would pay and the lowest price a seller would accept on a property.

**Maturity-** The date on which the principal balance of a loan, bond, or other financial instrument becomes due and payable. At the maturity of a 30-year loan the principal balance will be paid in full.

**Maximum financing-** The maximum amount a lender will lend on a specific loan program.

**Merged credit report-** A credit report that contains information from more than one credit-reporting agency. When the report is created, the information is compared for inconsistencies and duplicate entries. Any duplicates are combined to provide a summary of a your credit.

**Minimum payment-** The minimum amount that must be paid monthly on an account. On the HELOC product, the minimum payment is interest only during the draw period. On the Fixed Rate Second products, the minimum payment is principal and interest.

**Modification-** The act of changing any of the terms of the mortgage.

**Monthly debt-** A borrower's monthly expenses including credit cards, installment loans, student loan payments, alimony and child support and housing payment expense.

**Monthly mortgage insurance payment-** Portion of monthly payment that covers the cost of Private Mortgage Insurance.

**Monthly payment-** Payments to reduce the principal balance of a home loan made once a month.

**Monthly principal and interest payment-** Portion of monthly payment that covers the principal and interest due on the loan.

**Monthly taxes and insurance payment-** Portion of monthly payment that funds the escrow or impounds account for taxes and insurance.

**Mortgage-** A legal document that pledges a property to the lender as security for payment of a debt.

**Mortgage backed security-** A bond or other financial obligation secured by a pool of mortgage loans is called a Mortgage Backed Security (MBS).

**Mortgage banker-** A company that originates, sells and services mortgages exclusively for resale in the secondary mortgage market.

**Mortgage broker-** A company that originates but does not sell or service mortgages.

**Mortgage insurance-** A contract that insures the lender against loss caused by a borrower's default on a government mortgage or conventional mortgage. Mortgage insurance can be issued by a private company or by a government agency such as the Federal Housing Administration (FHA). Depending on the type of mortgage insurance, the insurance may cover a percentage of or virtually all of the mortgage loan.

**Mortgage insurance premium-** abr. MIP The amount paid by a borrower for mortgage insurance, either to a government agency such as the Federal Housing Administration (FHA) or to a private mortgage insurance (MI) company.

**Mortgage life insurance-** A type of term life insurance sometimes bought by borrowers. The amount of coverage decreases as the loan's principal balance declines. In the event that the borrower dies while the policy is in force, the debt is automatically satisfied by insurance proceeds.

**Mortgagee-** The lender in a mortgage agreement.

**Mortgagor-** The borrower in a mortgage agreement.

**Multi-dwelling units-** Properties that provide separate housing units for more than one family, although they secure only a single mortgage. Typically a 2-4 unit property.

**Negative amortization** - An increase in the outstanding balance of a mortgage that occurs when the monthly payment is not large enough to cover the interest due. The amount of the shortfall is added to the remaining balance to create "negative" amortization.

**Net cash flow-** The income that remains for an investment property after the monthly operating income is reduced by the monthly housing expense, which includes principal, interest, taxes, and insurance (PITI) for the mortgage, homeowners' association dues, leasehold payments, and subordinate financing payments.

**Net effective income-** The borrowers gross income minus taxes.

**Net worth-** The value of all of a person's assets, including cash, minus all liabilities.

**No closing cost loan-** A loan in which the fees the borrower(s) are not required to pay cash out-of-pocket at closing for the normal closing costs. The lender typically includes the closing costs in the principal balance or charges a higher interest rate than for a loan with closing costs to cover the advance of closing costs.

**No out of pocket cost loan-** A loan in which the borrower(s) are not required to pay cash out-of-pocket at closing for the normal closing costs. The lender typically includes the closing costs in the principal balance or charges a higher interest rate than for a loan with closing costs to cover the advance of closing costs.

**Non-conforming loan** - *See jumbo loan*

**Non-liquid asset-** An asset that cannot easily be converted into cash.

**Notary public-** one who is legally empowered to witness signatures, certify a document's validity, and to take depositions

**Note-** A legal document that obligates a borrower to repay a mortgage loan at a stated interest rate during a specified period of time.

**Note rate** - The interest rate stated on a mortgage note.

**Notice of default** - A formal written notice to a borrower that a default has occurred and that legal action may be taken.

**Offer** - An expression of willingness to purchase a property at a specified price.

**Open-end mortgage** - A type of mortgage that allows the homeowner to borrow additional money under the same mortgage, with certain conditions.

**Original principal balance** - The total amount of principal owed on a mortgage before any payments are made.

**Origination fee** - A fee paid to a lender for processing a loan application, making a home loan, and recording a mortgage against the borrower's real property as security for repayment of the loan. The origination fee is stated in the form of points (usually 1 to 5 points).

**Owner occupant** - A person who lives in a home he/she owns.

**Owner of record** - The individual named on a deed that has been recorded at the county recorders office.

**Partial payment** - A payment that is not sufficient to cover the scheduled monthly principal and interest payment on a mortgage loan.

**Payment change date** - The date when a new monthly payment amount takes effect on an adjustable rate mortgage (ARM). Generally, the payment change date occurs in the month immediately after the adjustment date and the borrower is notified 30 days prior as to the new rate.

**Payoff** - To pay the outstanding balance of a loan in full.

**Periodic payment cap** - A provision of an adjustable-rate mortgage (ARM) that limits how much the interest rate or loan payments may increase or decrease. In upward rate markets, it protects the borrower from large increases in the interest rate or monthly payment at each adjustment period.

**Periodic rate cap** - A provision of an adjustable-rate mortgage (ARM) that limits how much the interest rate or loan payments may increase or decrease. In upward rate markets, it protects the borrower from large increases in the interest rate or monthly payment at each adjustment period.

**Permanent buy down** - The borrower pays a loan fee or a seller Buy down to make a lower rate and lower payments for the duration of the loan.

**Personal property** - Any property that is not real property or is not permanently fixed to land. Cash, furniture, and cars are all examples of personal property.

**Piggyback mortgage** - A combination of two loans. Example: A loan is made for 100%% of the home price. 80%% of the purchase price is supplied by a 1st mortgage and 20%% by a 2nd mortgage. The 2nd mortgage is piggybacked since it's originated and closed at the same time as the 1st mortgage.

**PITI** - See: principal, interest, taxes, and insurance

**PITI reserves** - A cash amount that a borrower must have on hand after making a down payment and paying all closing costs for the purchase of a home. The principal, interest, taxes, and insurance (PITI) reserves must equal the amount that the borrower would have to pay for PITI for a predefined number of months.

**Point** - A point is 1%% of the amount of the mortgage loan amount (e.g., 1,000 on a $100,000 loan). See also Front Point, Back Point, and Discount Points.

**Portfolio loan** - A loan that is held as an investment by a bank or savings and loan instead of being sold on the secondary market to investors.

**Power of attorney** -A legal document authorizing one person to act on another's behalf. A power of attorney can grant complete authority or can be limited to certain acts and/or certain periods of time.

**Pre-approval-** A lender's conditional agreement to lend a specific amount on specific terms to a homebuyer. Sometimes a lender calls this an Upfront Approval or Approved.

**Pre-paid interest** - Mortgage interest that is paid in advance of when it is due.

**Pre-paid items -** Items required by lender to be paid at closing prior to the period they cover such as prorated property taxes, homeowners insurance and pre-paid interest.

**Pre-qualification** - The process of determining how much money a prospective home buyer might be eligible to borrow before he or she applies for a loan. When you pre-qualify, we ask you for information about your credit, assets and debts. Based on the information you provide and the loan type you want, the lender will calculate how large a loan you could qualify for. Please note that a pre-qualification is neither pre-approval nor a commitment to lend and requires you to submit additional information for review and approval.

**Pre-arranged refinancing agreement** - A formal or informal arrangement between a lender and a borrower where the lender agrees to offer special terms (such as a reduction in the rate or closing costs) for a future refinancing as an inducement for the borrower to enter into the original mortgage transaction.

**Pre-foreclosure sale** - A procedure in which the investor allows a mortgagor to avoid foreclosure by selling the property, typically for less than the amount that is owed to the lender.

**Prepayment** - Any amount paid to reduce the principal balance of a loan before the due date.

**Prepayment penalty** - A fee that may be charged to a borrower who pays off a loan before it is due. Generally, a prepayment penalty is added to a loan in exchange for a lower interest rate.

**Primary residence** - The place someone lives most of the time, as opposed to a 2nd or vacation home.

**Prime rate** - The interest rate that banks charge on short-term loans to its most creditworthy customers. Changes in the prime rate influence changes in other rates, including mortgage interest rates.

**Principal** - The amount borrowed or remaining unpaid. The part of the monthly payment that reduces the remaining balance of a mortgage.

**Principal balance** - The outstanding balance on a mortgage. The principal balance does not include interest or any other charges. See remaining balance.

**Principal payment** - Portion of your monthly payment that reduces the remaining balance of a home loan.

**Principal, interest, taxes, and insurance** - Four potential components of a monthly mortgage payment. Principal refers to the part of the monthly payment that reduces the remaining balance of the mortgage. Interest is the fee charged for borrowing money. Taxes and insurance refer to the amounts that may be paid into an escrow account each month for property taxes and mortgage and hazard insurance.

**Private mortgage insurance a.k.a. PMI.** - Mortgage insurance that is provided by a private mortgage insurance company to protect lenders against loss if a borrower defaults. Most lenders generally require PMI for a loan with a loan-to-value (LTV) percentage in excess of 80%%.

**Probate** - Court process to establish the validity of the will of a deceased person.

**Producer price index** - a.k.a. PPI. The monthly producer price index measures the level of prices for all goods produced and imported for sale in the primary marketplace. Increase in the PPI tends to lead other measures of inflation, which could cause the bond market to move down in price.

**Promissory note** - A written promise to repay a specified amount over a specified period of time.

**Property tax** - A tax based on the assessed value of a property. Tax rate is set on a county basis.

**Public auction** - A meeting in an announced public location to sell property to repay a mortgage that is in default.

**Purchase agreement** - A written contract signed by the buyer and seller stating the terms and conditions under which a property will be sold.

**Purchase money transaction** - A loan used in part as payment for a purchase. A loan that is used to buy a home is called a purchase money mortgage.

**Purchase price** - The total amount paid for a home.

**Qualifying ratios** - Calculations that are used in determining whether a borrower can qualify for a mortgage. They consist of two separate calculations: a housing expense as a percent of income ratio and total debt obligations as a percent of income ratio.

**Quiet title -** A legal action to resolve a dispute over title

**Quitclaim deed** - A deed that transfers, without warranty of ownership, whatever interest or title a grantor may have at the time the conveyance is made.

**Rate lock -** A commitment issued by a lender to a borrower guaranteeing a specified interest rate for a specified period of time.

**Rate reduction option** - A fixed-rate mortgage that includes a provision that gives the borrower an option to reduce the interest rate (without refinancing) at a later date. It is similar to a prearranged refinancing agreement, except that it does not require re-qualifying.

**Real estate agent** - A person who is normally licensed by the state and who, for a commission or a fee, assists in negotiating a real estate transaction.

**Real Estate Investment Trusts** - An investment trust that owns and manages a pool of commercial properties and mortgages and other real estate assets; shares can be bought and sold in the stock market.

**Real Estate Settlement Procedures Act** - Commonly known as RESPA, it is a consumer protection law that, among other things, requires advance disclosure of settlement costs to home buyers and sellers, prohibits certain types of referral and other fees, sets rules for escrow accounts, and requires notice to borrowers when servicing of a home loan is transferred.

**Real property** - Land and appurtenances, including anything of a permanent nature such as structures, trees, minerals, and the interest, benefits, and inherent rights thereof. Realtor A real estate broker or agent who holds active membership in a local real estate board that is affiliated with the National Association of Realtors.

**Recision** - The cancellation of a contract. When refinancing a mortgage on a principal residence RESPA gives the homeowner three days to cancel the mortgage contract.

**Re-conveyance** - A re-conveyance or deed of full re-conveyance removes the lien that the lender placed against the property when the loan was originally taken out. Thus, the lender conveys the property back to the owner.

**Recorder** - The public official who keeps records of transactions that affect real property in the area. Sometimes known as a "Registrar of Deeds" or "County Clerk."

**Recording** - The noting in a book of public record of the terms of a legal document affecting title to real property, such as a deed, a mortgage note, a satisfaction of mortgage, or an extension of mortgage.

**Recourse** - The right of the holder of a note secured by a mortgage or deed of trust to claim money from the borrower in default in addition to the property pledged as a collateral.

**Refinance transaction** - The process of obtaining a mortgage loan on a piece of property that you've already purchased, or paying off one loan with the proceeds from a new loan, typically using the same property as security for the new loan.

**Rehabilitation mortgage** - A mortgage created to cover the costs of repairing, improving, and sometimes acquiring an existing property.

**Remaining balance** - The amount of principal that has not yet been repaid.

**Remaining term** - The original amortization term minus the number of payments that have been applied.

**Rent with option to buy** -payment plan - An arrangement made to buy property by the seller on specific terms.

**Request for Notice of Default** - A recorded document that obligates the holder of the first mortgage lien to notify subordinate lien holders in the event of default by the borrower.

**Rescission**- The act of cancellation or annulment of a transaction or contract by the operation of a law. Borrowers usually have the option to cancel certain credit transactions, including a refinance or home equity transaction, within three business days after consummation (when the consumer becomes contractually obligated by, for example, signing the loan documents).

**Reverse mortgage** - A reverse mortgage is a special type of home loan that lets a homeowner convert a portion of the equity in his or her home into cash. The equity built up over years of home mortgage payments can be paid to you. But unlike a traditional home equity loan or second mortgage, no repayment is required until the borrower(s) no longer use the home as their principal residence. HUD's reverse mortgage provides these benefits, and it is federally insured as well.

**Revolving liability** - A credit arrangement, such as a credit card or HELOC, that allows a customer to borrow against a predetermined line of credit when purchasing goods and services. The borrower makes payments on the amount that is actually borrowed plus any interest due.

**Right of survivorship** - In joint tenancy, the right of survivors to acquire the interest of a deceased joint tenant.

**Rollover loan** - A loan that is amortized over a long period of time (e.g. 30 yrs) but the interest rate is fixed for a short period (e.g. 5 yrs). The loan may be extended or rolled over, at the end of the shorter term, based on the terms of the loan. Similar to an ARM.

**Rural Housing Service** - a.k.a. RHS. An agency within the Department of Agriculture. This agency provides financing to farmers and other qualified borrowers buying property in rural areas who are unable to obtain loans elsewhere. Funds are borrowed from the U.S. Treasury.

**Second home** - A property occupied part-time by a person in addition to his or her primary residence.

**Second mortgage** - A mortgage that has a lien position subordinate to the first mortgage.

**Secondary mortgage market -** An informal market where lenders and investors buy and sell existing mortgages. Government-sponsored entities and private investors buy mortgages from lenders who use the proceeds to make additional loans.

**Section 8** - The Section 8 program, which is the largest rent subsidy funding source of the Federal Government, provides funds to make up the difference between the housing a family can afford and the cost of housing in a specific area. The houses are privately owned. Landlords receive subsidies on behalf of qualified tenants, allowing the landlord to provide housing to low-income families and still receive fair market value for the rent.

**Secured loan** - A loan that is backed by collateral. If the borrower defaults, the lender can sell the collateral to satisfy the debt.

**Security** - The property that will be pledged as collateral for a loan. If the borrower defaults, the lender can sell the collateral to satisfy the debt.

**Security interest** - An interest a lender takes in the borrower's property to assure repayment of a debt. If the borrower defaults, the lender can sell the collateral to satisfy the debt.

**Seller take-back** - An agreement in which the owner of a property provides financing, often in combination with an assumable mortgage.

**Servicer** - An organization that collects principal and interest payments from borrowers and manages borrowers' tax and insurance escrow accounts. A mortgage banker is often paid a fee to service mortgages that have been purchased by an investor in the secondary mortgage market.

**Servicing** - The collection of principal and interest payments from borrowers and management of borrowers' tax and insurance escrow accounts.

**Settlement -** See   closing

**Settlement sheet** - also: HUD-1 settlement statement

**Sheriff's deed** - A deed given at the sheriff's sale in the foreclosure of a mortgage.

**Single-family residence** - Sometimes called an SFR or SFD, a single family residence is a residential structure designed with dwelling space for only one family.

**Special assessment** - A special tax imposed on property, individual lots or all property in the neighborhood to pay for improvements - street lights, sidewalks, etc.

**Special deposit account** - An account that is established for rehabilitation mortgages to hold the funds needed for the rehabilitation work so they can be disbursed from time to time as particular portions of the work are completed.

**Special warranty deed** - A special warranty deed is a deed of conveyance that contains one or more of the six warranties, but warranties are limited to only the extent that the loss is caused by an action of the grantor and not by the predecessors in title. The special warranty deed is the most commonly used form of conveyance between spouses when implementing the division of property made in a divorce decree.

**Stand alone** - A home equity loan originated without obtaining a first mortgage at the same time.

**Start rate** - See: initial interest rate

**Subordinate financing** - Any mortgage or other lien that has a priority that is lower than that of the first mortgage. The subordinate loan has a claim to payment in a foreclosure only after the first mortgage is paid.

**Subsidized second mortgage** - An alternative financing option known as the Community Seconds mortgage for low and moderate-income households. An investor purchases a first mortgage that has a subsidized second mortgage behind it. A state, county, or local housing agency, foundation, or nonprofit corporation may issue the second mortgage. Payment on the second mortgage is often deferred and carries a very low interest rate (or no interest rate).

**Survey** - A drawing or map showing the precise legal boundaries of a property, the location of improvements, easements, rights of way, encroachments, and other physical features.

**Sweat equity** - Contribution to the construction or rehabilitation of a property in the form of labor or services performed personally by the owner.

**Tax lien** - Lien for nonpayment of taxes.

**Tax sale** - Public sale of a property at an auction by a government authority as a result of non-payment of taxes.

**Tenancy at will** - A tenancy at will is created when the tenant enters the dwelling with the landlords consent, for an indefinite amount of time, and with no express provisions governing rent. The tenant may decide to leave the property at any time or must leave at the landlord's will.

**Tenancy by the entirety** - A type of joint tenancy of property that provides right of survivorship and is available only to a husband and wife. One spouse dies the property goes to the other spouse. Contrast with tenancy in common and joint tenancy.

**Tenancy for years** - Tenancy for years is a tenancy measured by a period of time, lasting for an amount of time specified in the lease. Unless the lease provides otherwise, no notice is necessary to terminate such a tenancy.

**Tenancy in common** - A type of joint tenancy in a property without right of survivorship. Contrast with tenancy by the entirety and with joint tenancy.

**Tenancy in severalty** - Ownership of property vested in one person alone, and not held jointly with another; also called Several Tenancy or Sole Tenancy.

**Third-party origination** - A process by which a lender uses another party to completely or partially originate, process, underwrite, close, fund, or package the home loan.

**Title** - A legal document evidencing a person's right to or ownership of a property.

**Title Company** - A company that specializes in examining and insuring titles to real estate.

**Title insurance** - Insurance that protects the lender (lender's policy) or the buyer (owner's policy) against loss arising from disputes over ownership of a property.

**Title search** - A check of the title records to ensure that the seller is the legal owner of the property and that there are no liens or other claims outstanding.

**Total expense ratio** - Total obligations as a percentage of gross monthly income. The total expense ratio includes monthly housing expenses plus other monthly debts. Used to help qualify a potential borrower for a home loan.

**Total monthly payment** - Amount paid each month that covers all of PITI (principal, interest, taxes, and insurance).

**Town house** - Residence which normally has 2 or more floors and is attached to other similar units. Town houses are commonly found in planned unit developments (PUDs) and condominiums.

**Tract -** A parcel of land, generally held for subdividing.

**Transaction fee** - A fee charged each time the borrower draws on the credit line.

**Transfer of ownership** - Any means by which the ownership of a property changes hands. Lenders consider all of the following situations to be a transfer of ownership: the purchase of a property "subject to" the mortgage, the assumption of the mortgage debt by the property purchaser, and any exchange of possession of the property under a land sales contract or any other land trust device. In cases in which an inter vivos revocable trust is the borrower, lenders also consider any transfer of a beneficial interest in the trust to be a transfer of ownership.

**Transfer tax** - State or local tax payable when title to a property passes from one owner to another.

**Treasury index** - An index that is used to determine interest rate changes for certain adjustable-rate mortgage (ARM) plans. It is based on the results of auctions that the U.S. Treasury holds for its Treasury bills and securities or is derived from the U.S. Treasury's daily yield curve, which is based on the closing market bid yields on actively traded Treasury securities in the over-the-counter market.

**Trust account** - A separate bank account maintained by a broker or escrow company to handle all money collected for clients. A broker may not commingle these funds with his own funds.

**Trustee** - A fiduciary who holds or controls property for the benefit of another.

**Truth-in-Lending** - A federal law that requires lenders to fully disclose, in writing, the terms and conditions of credit, such as a mortgage, including the annual percentage rate (APR) and other charges. Sometimes called TiL, Regualation Z, or a RegZ.

**Underwriting** - The process of evaluating a loan application to determine the risk involved for the lender. Underwriting involves an analysis of the borrower's creditworthiness and the quality of the property itself.

169

**Undivided interest** - Two or more persons who hold title to real property without indicating each party's interests by percentage or description of a portion of the real estate.

**Unsecured loan** - A loan that is not backed by collateral.

**Usury - 1)** an exorbitant or unlawful rate of interest 2) the act of lending money at an exorbitant rate of interest

**VA mortgage** - A mortgage that is guaranteed by the Department of Veterans Affairs (VA). Also known as a government mortgage.

**Variable rate** - An interest rate that changes periodically in relation to an index. Payments may increase or decrease per the terms of the loan agreement or note.

**Variable rate mortgage** - a.k.a. VRM *See*  adjustable rate mortgage

**Verification of Deposit** - A Verification of Deposit (VOD) is a document signed by the borrower's bank or other financial institution verifying the account balance and history. Usually required by lenders to verify borrower has the amount of money he/she claims on the 1003.

**Verification of Employment** - A Verification of Employment (VOE) is a document signed by the borrower's employer verifying his/her starting date, job title, salary, probability of continued employment and probability of future overtime.

**Veterans Affairs, Department of** - An agency of the federal government that guarantees residential mortgages made to eligible veterans of the military services. The guarantee protects the lender against loss and thus encourages lenders to make mortgages to veterans.

**Waiver** - The voluntary renunciation, abandonment, or surrender of some claim, right, or privilege.

**Wraparound mortgage** - Wraparound mortgages are a way to allow buyers to purchase a home without having to qualify for a loan or to pay closing costs. The contract is made between the buyer and seller with the lender approval. The seller continues to pay the existing loan while the buyer pays the seller for the new 'wraparound' loan. Wraparounds are subordinate to all existing mortgages. It is important for the seller to obtain lender's approval or the lender may enforce the acceleration clause in the existing mortgage.

**Year-end statement** - A report sent to the borrower each year. The report shows how much was paid in taxes and interest during the year, as well as the remaining mortgage loan balance at the end of the year.

**Yield spread premium** - YSP is a premium paid to loan originators and mortgage brokers in exchange for them originating a loan at a higher than market interest rate. Depending on the lender, the amount of the loan, current market conditions, and the "spread" (that is, the difference between the par rate and the rate used), this premium can amount to thousands of dollars per transaction.

**Zoning** - dividing an area into zones or sections reserved for different purposes such as residence, business, and manufacturing, etc...

CPSIA information can be obtained
at www.ICGtesting.com
Printed in the USA
BVOW10s2249260416
445738BV00007B/39/P